CHRISTIANITY

AND

MODERN PAGANISM

THE KNUBEL-MILLER LECTURES — 1959

Christianity and Modern Paganism

By

Lawrence D. Folkemer

Board of Publication
of the United Lutheran Church in America

Philadelphia

DEDICATED

to my wife

L.D.F.

TABLE OF CONTENTS

FOREWORD

This series of lectures originally started out to deal exclusively with the Christian mission in the non-Christian, other-believing world, and even more specifically with the great non-Christian faiths. Had the original plan been carried out, there would have appeared in these pages a fuller doctrinal exposition of Christianity and other religions. That will have to wait for a later time. It was felt that the purpose of the Knubel-Miller lectures could be served better by dealing with paganism in a broader sense, to include not only the religious but the irreligious pagan world. The former has its center of operation in places distant from American shores; the latter thrives all around us and, as we shall see, in our very midst. But the modern world being what it is, that is, an ever shrinking world, in which, if I may paraphrase John Donne, no land or religion is an island unto itself, no form of modern paganism can be considered of only casual interest to the concerned Christian. And in the light of our Lord's Great Commission we must forever be preoccupied with the "Gospel Conquest" of the world. Indeed, if this book had a text it would be the most familiar of all: ". . . God so loved the *world*."

The reader, therefore, is bidden to don bifocals, that with one lens he may see the paganism in the distance (though never far away), and with the other he may look upon it at close range. The figure of speech is not altogether inappropriate for there is an underlying unity to the World

Mission of the Church even when the Church must give thorough and intelligent attention to this twofoldness of paganism.

To those sixty-one missionaries and national Christian leaders, who patiently worked through sixteen comprehensive essay questions submitted to them by the writer, in what amounted to a "small-sized edition" of a philosophy of missions, may I express my profound respect and gratitude. Missionaries are literally the "salt of the earth" and the "light of the world." Their work "on the frontiers" is becoming an increasingly more difficult assignment. My personal thanks go also to Dr. Earl Erb, Executive Secretary of the Board of Foreign Missions, United Lutheran Church in America, through whose good graces overseas communications with missionaries were made possible.

A word of appreciation is reserved for the Board of Higher Education of the United Lutheran Church in America which is the steward of the Knubel-Miller Foundation Lectures; for those committee members at the lecture places whose arrangements and promotion secured a good response, and for the hundreds of pastors and concerned laymen who not only heard the lectures but by their many questions and much discussion, made the experience a fruitful one for me. To my typists, my secretary, Mrs. Komenda, and Mrs. Slater, a friend and member of my congregation, my thanks.

May, 1959   Lawrence D. Folkemer

1

THE GREAT ECUMENICAL PROBLEM

This lecture is being written in a New York hotel in early December to the accompaniment of an electronic device blaring forth carols for mass pleasure (and business receipts!). "Joy to the world the Lord is come . . . Let every heart prepare him room."

The irony is that there is scarcely "room" for the carol itself to be heard. With thousands rushing in and out of New York office buildings and shoppers pushing their way through department stores, with taxis and trucks screeching to a stop and shrill horns blowing, with traffic whistles piercing the din, this electronic entertainer appears to cater only to its own amusement. Parrot-like, it mechanically plays to itself like an introverted, imprisoned church presiding over its own sanctuary and praying "with itself." Life rushes on down below, faintly conscious of the melodies from above, but most of the time so intent on the business at hand, the destinations to be reached, that the good ear is to the ground and the deaf ear raised. And between the ears there is not much communication! The music is not getting through. There is joy for the world in his coming, but not much room.

The Gospel is addressed to the world, not to rescue as many out of it as time permits but to redeem them within and into it that the world itself may be saved. But there is a vast indifference to the Gospel both within and outside of Christendom. The "Christendom illusion" that we live in a converted Christendom must be shattered before we can discover the secret of reaching the unconvinced with the Gospel. Paul Evdokinov makes the striking comment: "We cannot say the Gospel comes up against a stone wall, for a wall is hard and resistant and that is a reaction. The Gospel meets with supreme indifference." [1] The Gospel is aimed at this world, a world created, preserved and already redeemed. The Good News which came from beyond this world exists for the world. But the world is indifferent. It is most likely to say quietly to the Gospel, "so what?" Quietly, for it is not hostile so much as unmindful. "He was in the world, and the world was made through him, yet the world knew him not." [2] Modern substitutes for the Gospel may turn out to be only hirelings leaving the world a shepherdless flock; but the Gospel itself seems presently not to be a live option.

Gospel indifference, however, is not synonymous with religious inactivity. There is much religious excitement. A friend recently invited me to speak to his "cultural study group." "We have talked about painting and pottery and politics," he said, "but we haven't had anyone yet 'discuss religion.' And that would make a delightful subject!" Especially delightful if the conversation is left wide open and no one suggests making a decision. Religion is surefire and downright popular. Ask any vendor of paperbacks. Old Testament scholars who but a few years ago had to content themselves with a select audience of professional devotees now find their scholarship saleable as shoppers browse over the *Dead Sea Scrolls* shoulder to shoulder with admirers of Perry Mason. Signs of religious interest are too commonplace and marked to draw further comment. And it must be stated that the interest is not altogether superficial. We must not discredit the interest even when it is uncritical and

---

[1] *Ecumenical Review,* Autumn, 1949, p. 23.
[2] John 1:10.

utilitarian. Some "rice" Christians become real Christians.
A recent fetish has grown up in periodicals and pulpits to
badger the wave of religious enthusiasm. Sober and dis-
cerning we must be in our judgment, but not irresponsible
iconoclasts. Much of the contemporary interest in religion
is quite serious and runs on into deeper channels of self-
scrutiny and application. One compensation, at least, of a
shattered world is that true faith finds the kind of opportunity
that scepticism enjoys in less trammeled times.

But the basic question still persists. What room is there
in the world for the Gospel? Scattered islands of individual
rescue there are (add up the decisions for Christ!) but how
deeply, with all the religious activity, has the Word pene-
trated into the knotty fabric of modern society? As a recent
study sheet (May, 1958) of the Department of Evangelism
of the World Council of Churches suggests, the real implications of the Gospel for a world in catastrophic change, both
East and West, are far from worked out. Increased personal
pietism and conversions are largely irrelevant to these
problems. The "rescued" are often evangelically ineffective
in their own cultural spheres. The world remains hardshell.

This leads to a third observation about the world which
the Gospel confronts. It is a world of rapid change, confusion
and conflict. Each demands a more profound analysis than
these lectures can provide, but they stand in close relationship. Changes of the last decade have been little short of
catastrophic. The breakthroughs in science, for example,
while offering boons beyond imagination have more than
balanced their gifts with frightful explorations that have
delivered the breakdown of confidence and hope. Men and
nations can no longer afford to trust each other. And with
the change has come confusion.

Scientists themselves are by no means united about the
present and future effects of global and outer space scientific

activity. Competent specialists are still lined up on opposite sides of the problem of radioactive fallout. International tension has only served to put scientists in competitive rather than cooperative relationships. Paradoxically, the god of scientific objectivity is made to genuflect before intensely subjective national consciousness and loyalty. This tragic dilemma is a matter of great professional and personal concern for the sensitive scientist. Science has made the deepest of all invasions into human history and the world is frightened. Some feel that the possibility of mutual annihilation is deterrent enough. But thinking men are unconvinced. Safeguards are never adequate against fools and monsters. National leaders boast of "postures of strength" in military and missile strategy. They are postures only of fear and futility.

But scientific changes are not the only sources of confusion and conflict. To mention but a few: the well-financed and cleverly contrived advertising campaigns for the mass manipulation of the public which so dehumanizes men as to make them objects rather than persons; the emotionally inflammatory developments in race relations which bedevil a society tragically unprepared to face them; a redirection of educational philosophy conditioned largely by fast-moving developments in science and technology; and in the area of religion, the rivalries, tensions, and fragmentations within Christianity (notwithstanding the movements toward unity and cooperation), and the critical confrontation of Christianity with the great non-Christian faiths of the East as well as the encounter with the godless and secular ideologies of the West. This brief listing of what actually mounts up to a prolific catalogue of changes in what prosaically is termed "the new age" barely suggests the background for confusion and conflict in the human soul and society of our time. And all of it poses serious problems for the Gospel and the Church established to communicate the Gospel to men.

Since this lecture series is concerned in part with the Christian encounter with Eastern faiths, an extended comment on revolutionary changes now in progress in the East is necessary. A stepped-up, highly concentrated study tour of the Far and Near East hardly qualifies anyone to speak too boldly about revolutionary developments in Asia, but certain facts become evident after extensive conversations with political and religious leaders, both Christian and non-Christian. The impact of Western culture is obvious and admitted. The influence of Christianity upon religious and broader sociological developments is not inconsiderable. The revolution is exciting, even though ominous.

The charge of "neutralism" leveled by the West against the East, particularly India, and later silenced, looks quite different when seen through Southeast Asian eyes. For one thing, communism is not viewed from the reference point of Christian faith in this non-Christian portion of the world. And though it may be argued with validity that much of the Communist ideology and method run counter to basic presuppositions of oriental religion and culture, the East chooses to deal with the menace in its own fashion and as it relates to its own situation, without regard to the balance of power in the western world. The East resents the implication of unconcern for principle and moral integrity in the charge of neutralism. Asians are little interested in having their national policies determined by London, Moscow or Washington. A newly-discovered pride in things native has engendered a widespread hope and national sense of destiny. That destiny seems achievable only in peace and non-alignment with western power blocs.

The Far and Near East fairly bristle with progress plans. India is well along in its second five-year plan of national reforms. Other nations are plunging into rural, urban, and industrial programs as well as educational and health plans in order to assume as quickly as possible their role in the destiny of the modern world. Intense subsidized recruitment schemes for producing qualified leaders are in operation. These, not religion, are the interests which absorb the primary attention of Asians.

The East is riding the high wave of nationalism. It is an all-encompassing nationalism—political, economic, cultural, and religious. Looked at hopefully, it is the assertion by a people of their own national self-consciousness and individuality in relation to other peoples which may one day find a higher fulfillment in true world community. Less hopefully, it may become at least for a generation strongly introvertive, suspicious and disdainful of other cultures and faiths. The latter appears uppermost at the present time. The ecumenical task of the Church is to study the nature of this complex situation in Asia from the perspective of Christian responsibility, but that perspective must be broad enough to measure the sincere aspirations of the non-Christian Asian mentality.

The entire East is in the throes of a cultural crisis. The large-scale adoption of cultural values from the West has negated many of the traditional native values and, paradoxically, has emphasized the need for their conservation and reinterpretation. The Bangkok Conference (1950) of Asian Christian leaders made a penetrating analysis of this cultural dilemma and called upon the Church in Asia to interpret the Christian message, by word and deed, in a manner truly relevant to the situation. The impact of the twentieth century world on the traditional world of the East poses herculean tasks and calls up profound, courageous Christian leadership and witness.[3] It is not only the Eastern faiths, therefore, that the Gospel and its bearers face, but the whole troubled, un-redeemed world of the East. Walter Van Kirk, at the Assembly of the World Christian Mission in Toronto (1952) brought the matter into sharp focus when he said:

"There comes a time in the history of humans when aspirations for larger living, long suppressed, become articulate and overpowering, when the concept of divine justice, however divinely conceived, leavens the imagination and behavior of God's people everywhere; when the barriers to the fulfillment of man's higher destiny are broken down either by peaceful processes or by revolutionary violence. Such a time has come for peoples of Asia and Africa. The Communists did not open the eyes of the people. The Communists did not set these people marching. It is the spirit of the living and eternal God that has engendered among these people the hope of social and economic justice. Nor are the masses of the underdeveloped areas in revolt against the West. They are in revolt against the tyranny of poverty, famine, disease and deprivation. They do not believe it was intended they should forever walk in rags along the deadend road of frustration."[4]

Some dynamic, creative center of integration must be found for this cultural crisis in Asia—as indeed, it must be discovered in the West—and experience makes it highly doubtful whether any narrowly national or regional interests and loyalties will resolve what is at root a spiritual need. Where is cultural deliverance to be found? For New India, Mr. Radhakrishnan, Vice-President of India, sees it in a reborn and reinterpreted Hinduism. World Buddhist thinkers are

[3] *Ecumenical Review*, April, 1953, p. 253.
[4] Quoted from *Japan Christian Quarterly*, Autumn, 1952, p. 281.

equally convinced that the solution is in a revived Buddhist conception of reality and action. If I understand him aright, Professor F. S. Northrup of Yale University pleads for a comprehensive, creative religious synthesis that will harmonize the diverse religious traditions of East and West, conserve the living beliefs of all religions and so produce a cosmic "team effort" that will put to rout materialism and secularism. The Apostle Paul was bold enough to say that "God was in Christ reconciling the world unto himself." Not as a pulpit slogan piously proclaimed without regard for the complexity of the cultural crisis, but the Gospel in Christ carefully articulated, and carried with wisdom and commitment to the very center and along all the borders of human society.

Now quite aside from the solutions proposed, the real point we are making is that the task of world redemption involves a thorough understanding of the world as it is. No amount of religious revival of itself is adequate. It may totally miss the mark by creating a smokescreen of religiosity. What is called for is not religious sparring but world wrestling and encounter. The fallacy of fundamentalism lies not so much in its theology as in its obsession with theology and its unconcern for the world other than to denounce it. The world either does not hear the denunciation or does not understand it. The ecumenical task of the Church remains essentially the same for West and East. The problem is not that of missions but *Mission*. Somehow it must be made manifest in Asia that the Christian community, out of divine obedience, is profoundly concerned about the nations themselves, their aspirations, problems, sufferings, and temptations, their cultural crisis. A curious belief has arisen, at home and abroad, that for a person to accept the Christian way weakens his value as a citizen, separates him from the critical issues, and disqualifies him from participation in the reshaping of the social and political life of the nation. How much of this is the result of the tragic lack of a Christian concept of citizenship?

This is a world, too, in which important lines of communication have been severed.[5] Communication is a magic word today and greatly overworked, but it is an obvious fact nonetheless that great tragedies lie in ruptured relations. The dissolution of marriage vows, the collapse of family ties, the rifts in education, the moral breakdown in community, the disharmony among races, the confusion of national policies, the conflict between national cultures and the stalemate and retrogression in international affairs, all reflect the cosmic division in the one world Almighty God created. The Church itself offers no exception. The failure of the pulpit to reach and activate the pew accounts in part for the failure of the pew to change the community. Each department of life sets up its own rigid autonomy: politics, industry, the arts, education, and religion. And the lines of communication between them are broken.

Underneath all this there is a spiritual homesickness in the heart. Mankind lives in a spiritual twilight. For some, it is the gathering darkness before the end. Others choose to hope that it is the darkness that precedes the dawn. Must it get darker before the light? Is the poet correct in saying that we need the darkness for the sake of humility and the sense of need in order to see our salvation? There is a groping and nostalgia in the soul. Many have lost the way and even the idea that there is a way. Yet there is a yearning for meaning among those who will not be content with perpetual loose ends; and a search for community by those who long to be "real persons." Mankind with all its stumbling has not lost

---

[5] Three small books are worth study: Hendrik Kraemer, *Communication of the Christian Faith;* David Read, *Communication and Christian Faith,* and Malcolm Boyd, *Crisis in Communication.*

its hunger for salvation and an anchorage for its deepest hopes. But where will it seek salvation and hope?

Ecumenical problem stated

Since its beginning, the ecumenical movement has concerned itself primarily with the problem of unity. This was essential. Unity is inherent in the Gospel and divisiveness is the very antithesis of the New Testament message of spiritual community. Ruptures had to be repaired. So churchmen of all traditions gave serious attention to restudy of the Scriptures, particularly with regard to the meaning of the Church. The fruit of that study is abundantly manifest in the solid fact of a World Council of Churches and a continuing growth in Christian koinonia. When the Holy Spirit is granted leadership of the Church and men listen, marvelous things happen. Man-imposed obstructions fall away one after another. Unity becomes more than a dream, it takes on reality. And the greater things are yet to be.

But the preoccupation of the Church with its problem of unity, essential as it was and is, prevented it from tackling the equally urgent problem of the universality of the Gospel. While the Church busied itself with its internal life, the world slipped farther from the grasp of the Gospel. Two worlds fell away really: the world it thought it held— Christendom—though it never did; and the world it hoped to secure for the Gospel from centuries-old competitors. The one world, though nominally Christian, enthroned an assortment of idolatrous substitutes; the other world rejuvenated its gods and made audacious new claims for their superiority. The authority and universality of the Gospel was laid on the block. The titanic struggle now rests between a universal Gospel and a diversified formidable paganism. How may the Christian community effectually convince both an idolatrous and a religious paganism that their redemption lies in the Gospel of God. Or, to phrase it in biblical terms, how may the words of the Apostles John and Paul, "For God so loved the world that he gave his only son, that whoever believes in him should not perish but have eternal life," and "God was in Christ reconciling the world unto himself," be globally realized? If the words "Gospel" and "ecumenical" mean anything, they mean bringing the whole world under the dominion of our Lord.

This can hardly be thought of as *an* ecumenical problem; it is the most contemporarily-crucial one ever laid in the lap of the Catholic Church of Christ. The task has not been made easier in these last two decades by the rampant spread of communism and secularism (in both East and West) or by the all-embracing cultural-political-religious nationalism of the non-Christian world. The problem is considerably greater than one of evangelism in the usual rendering of the term. It is philosophical, theological and cultural.

Opposition to the Gospel has become more formidable and subtle than ever before, calling for an encounter simultaneously on two fronts. The issue is greater than that of competing religions doing theological battle with one another. It is the conflict between the Word and the world; the Truth in Christ the Way, the Truth, and the Life and the hunger, search and oftimes repudiation of that Truth in the world. Because the Christian Church presents and represents the Gospel in the unchristian and non-Christian world, the Gospel itself may become the casualty along with the Church constituted to propagate and embody it.

Edmund Perry, in *The Gospel in Dispute,* sees three factors threatening the Gospel conquest of the world. One is the disturbing fact that the entire geographical world has been turned into a vast mission field. The Gospel can scarcely be said to hold sovereignty anywhere. As Christianity once conquered the pagan world of Rome and created her own culture, she now must reconquer the culture she largely created, as well as the dynamically religious and aggressive non-Christian world. Speaking before the Division of Foreign Missions of the National Council of Churches in early December, 1958, Dr. Wilson of Church World Service deplored the lack of cross-fertilization between home and foreign mission agencies: "I do not think it foolish that we should request missionaries from our sister churches overseas as they are requested from ours in order to help us meet problems of race relations and secularism in this country." To borrow from Wesley, the entire world is the parish of the Gospel. We can speak no less of Mission U.S.A. than Mission India or Africa. The problem is global and parochial. It is as narrow as every single Christian parish and its community (and every soul that makes up that parish), and as broad as the far-flung reaches of the globe.

A second factor threatening the Gospel is a deep impediment within the Western Church itself. R. Pierce Beaver comments that the missionary enterprise has been proceeding for the "past two centuries on the basis of a few simple, generally held, but unformulated assumptions." What is demanded is "a new understanding of the nature of the mission and a set of principles derived from a study of the ministry of the Church in the contemporary situation in the light of the teaching of the Bible, theology, and history. No new developments in the realm of organization or methods can equal in importance this search for basic principles." [6] There is considerable indecisiveness and divisiveness of thought on what constitutes the Christian mission, its authority and motive. Our own United Lutheran Church Board of Foreign Missions recently drafted an eminently worthwhile and progressive statement of policy on the

[6] *Chicago Theological Seminary Register,* November, 1952.

world-wide mission of proclaiming the Gospel. Its formulation reflected the broad experience of the missionaries themselves and was no product of a Madison Avenue office chair. But it was a statement primarily of policy and missionary procedures and only by scant reference and implication touched upon the fundamentally urgent need of a theology and philosophy of Mission.

A quarter of a century has passed since the publication of the highly controversial, so-called Laymens' Report, *Rethinking Missions*, which the churches have largely, and I think, justly, repudiated in the Missionary Councils of Tambaram (1938), Whitby (1947), and Willingen (1952), as well as the two Assemblies of the World Council of Churches in Amsterdam (1948) and Evanston (1954), but there still remains considerable confusion of thought and practice in the philosophy of Mission. At the present time some of the greatest theological and missiological minds of our generation, both Eastern and Western, are fastened upon this question and some brilliant insights have resulted. One precautionary comment is offered for what it is worth. The problem is complex and demands more than the labors of theological specialists. So does the problem of post-Christian paganism in Mission U.S.A. Issues are broadly cultural, involving political, economic and sociological factors. No "purely religious" solution is adequate. No simple or even highly theologized "give them Christ" solution is the answer.

The third factor, according to Perry, threatening the Christian mission today is the "resurgence of religion" and the renascence of religions in West and East. We have already made reference to the large scale religious activity in the West. Looking at it most optimistically, interest in Christianity and the Church could be a preparation for the way of the Gospel to the world. There must be no disparagement of the interest where it is genuine. But the fashionable parade of religion down Main Street sports a strange medley of banners. God is, at times, as vague as the crooner's Man Upstairs and as "pally" as a "good American Daddy." Or He is turned into a cosmic bellhop answering all calls for peace, security and, if not too presumptuous, prosperity! Prayer becomes a daily prescription for "subjective release" (never mind the object!) while the Kingdom is not too different from the democratic process and the American way of life." The Christian experience is often indistinguishable from a general religious feeling. Faith in faith substitutes for trust in the God of our Lord Jesus Christ. Much of the current religious enthusiasm is admittedly a fiasco.

But the real obstacle lies in a religious faith that seems bonafide enough but is irrelevant and inapplicable to the world; while we have become more pious we also have become more secularistic. Paradoxically, a world which has become seemingly more religious has moved farther away from redemption.

There is a considerable parallel to this western interest in religion in the renascence of religions of the East. Much of it is just as superficial as it is in the West. Orientals are learning, too, how to promote religion. Interest has undoubtedly been stimulated by freshly-won political independence and the desire to revive all things endemic to the culture. It has been fed certainly by apprehensions over the progress and influence of Christian missionary activity. Any "imported" religion, in their eyes, given too generous hospitality may subtly open the gate to a cultural imperialism like the political and economic imperialism from which they have only recently revolted. It is said that Gandhi's championing of the cause of the outcastes, largely restricted by the rigid laws of caste, was not a little stimulated by his fear lest they be lost to Christianity. Cultural imperialism is a far more subtle, less obvious threat than political and economic imperialism. Professor Northrup points out: "If one conquers a people politically and exploits them economically, while leaving their basic religious and philosophical beliefs intact, one has restrained and harmed their bodies but has not touched their spirit or their souls. When, however, by missionary effort, one shifts them from their traditional basic religious and philosophical beliefs, one destroys their cultural and spiritual tradition in soul as well as body." [7] It may be added that it is not yet completely clear how, if the East should become Christian, its cultural traditions may not suffer irreparable damage. One may reason, as indeed the Christian must, that the cultural traditions will find their richest fulfillment through the redemptive work of the Gospel, but to the Oriental it is not self-evident.

Some of our Lutheran missionaries have been keenly observant on this point of cultural imperialism. To seek to impose or to continue the imposition of western thought forms other than those which have been eagerly chosen, would be to make the East a cultural garden transplanted from the West. Independence has arrested that trend and a universal enthusiasm for an indigenous Christianity has reshaped the Christian mission. The latter is already well along in its course. The passion for indigeneity stirs up other questions which we shall discuss later but of the impropriety and wrongness of an imposed culture there can be no doubt.

Yet there is another kind of imperialism, if you please, the imperialism of the Gospel, which is neither western nor eastern but a vertical shaft thrust into the center of all culture to redeem it. It is at once a judgment and fulfillment of a particular culture. This imperialism is not imposed. By nature it cannot be any more imposed than the Gospel can. But wherever the Gospel is received, its imperial design pro-

[7] *Christian Century,* September 14, 1955.

duces change like leaven in the lump. A young African missionary skillfully describes this Gospel yeast in the Loma culture. It is necessary to quote at some length.

"As we interpret Christianity supraculturally—we find in it the element of individual responsibility, first for our conduct before God and then before our fellows. Briefly, this emphasis on individual responsibility has led to placing priority on individual rights and individual initiative. It has helped to create an atmosphere favorable to a certain kind of law, a certain kind of society, and a certain kind of economic system.

"The idea of individual responsibility stands in contrast to the Loma idea of dependency. The Christian evangelist says in all honesty that he is not advocating a change in this idea (i.e., the Loma idea of dependency) because of its inadequacy for his own legal, social, or economic system, but because it is not harmonious with the Christian idea (of the Gospel).

. . . "Or take the idea of work. We believe that God made and gave us the world to use and take care of—to work with, in other words. There is not only an opportunity here, but a responsibility as well. Moreover, we believe that we can show our gratitude to God and praise him and love him by carrying out our responsibilities. So as Christians we place a high value in work, as a means of obeying God's will and glorifying his name.

. . . "This idea of work is in contrast to the Loma idea. As far as we can understand it, the Loma idea of work is to do as little as possible. This is not to be interpreted, I think, as the conclusion of lazy men, but of a practical point of view that has a great many aspects (that I will not go into now).

"If, however, we try to share the Christian idea of work as we see it, we are likely to share as well an atmosphere that produces the cultural phenomena of our economics, education and science."

Our missionary friend follows this line of reasoning into a number of other areas and is particularly illuminating in her discussion of time and history, both with respect to the Gospel and Loma culture:

"To a Christian, time is of the essence. The New Testament is made dynamic with a sense of time. In the fullness of time came the Messiah. The harvest is ripe now for the cutting. The day of judgment *is* at hand. Work while it *is* day, for the night comes . . . The Christian idea of time is in conspicuous contrast to the Loma idea of time. The Loma people largely ignore divisions of time.

"The idea of time can be extended to the most important one of history. Christianity is imbued with a sense of history . . . Christ did indeed come in history . . . He left us with the message of his second coming (to fulfill history). He left us also with the command to extend the Kingdom and prepare for the day of his coming.

"And so our life anticipates the morrow. We make plans and work for improvements. Again, this idea of history represents a new color in the Loma spectrum. As far as I can understand, they have compressed history and the future into an eternal present. Not only is there no recognition of the history of event, there is no such thing as a plan for any remote tomorrow; and the standard for achievement of a Loma man lies in meeting the level of his father, not in surpassing it." [8]

To teach the Loma people the Christian meaning of history would be to sow "the seeds for a basic change in culture." This is an imperialism stemming from the

---

[8] The quotations are taken from replies to sixteen essay questions sent to sixty missionaries representing all parts of the United Lutheran Church mission fields.

Gospel which is uncontrollable, granted the full acceptance of the Gospel itself. To witness to the Gospel is the missionary's responsibility. "Constant self-examination will preserve the missionary from any imperialism other than the imperialistic interests of God."

Another missionary, a doctor, boldly asserts the difference the Gospel makes in the conduct of a hospital. And it runs head-on in conflict with a cultural presupposition. "Without direction" [the phase implies "without Gospel presupposition"] . . . "men would be served first—women and children last, friends and local politicians would get favored treatment—all remnants of tribal experience and ways of thinking." But the Gospel, in its universal concern for all individuals, irrespective of sex and station in society and, more importantly, with its accent on selflessness and sacrifice, places a value judgment upon the old culture and gives it a new direction by an imperialism of the spirit.

The deeper cause for the renascence of the old faiths is to be found in an internal dissatisfaction with religious traditionalism itself and an apprehension over the definite trend toward secularism, as much an affliction in the East as in the West. More so, perhaps, because in the East religion virtually monopolized culture, so that with the acceptance of the western scientific and industrial revolution religion lost hold of contemporary life. It was left isolated and out of reach of the currents of thought. If it were to remain alive at all the religion of the fathers must be more than revitalized. It must be reinterpreted to withstand the pressures of modernism and give direction and soul to a world newly created. Radhakrishnan's efforts to rethink Hinduism must be evaluated in that context.

The rejuvenation of the non-Christian faiths, in turn, intensifies the conflict for Christianity and the Gospel. Yet this is not wholly an occasion for solicitude. Christians live in the faith that the Gospel of God is sufficient for the salvation of all men and all culture. No one may presume to limit the power of the Holy Spirit. In addition, just such a renascence of the old faiths may refine the Church's witness and enable it more truly to understand its own faith and then more truly estimate and intelligently deal with the vigorously religious world that calls the Gospel into dispute.

Pagan counteraction

The Missionary Council of Willingen observed that not since the seventh century when Christianity stood confronted by the ominous spread of Islam, have the message and strategy of the Christian mission been so searchingly tested and tried. That was 1952. The intervening seven years have not only substantiated that comment but heightened the fact. Many predicted that with the rapid spread of secular interests, and as the various revolutions in economics, politics, and technology gathered force, the collapse of Buddhism, Hinduism, and Islam, as living religions would follow. An American general confidently and openly appealed for a thousand Christian missionaries to come to Japan to Christianize the land during this most auspicious period. The prophecies were not only false, but wrong in character. They savored too much of the spirit of imperialism. Asia has not been gripped by such feverish religious activity for centuries. Movements of revival, reform and reinterpretation are increasing at a rapid pace.

The striking thing is that the revival is turning into revolt. The revolt against Western domination is justifiable and against Western culture understandable. It is the revolt against Christianity which is somewhat baffling to the Christian, especially since there is undeniable evidence (often admitted) of Christian influence, direct or indirect, in the great awakening of Asia.[9] Why the antagonism to Christianity, in particular its evangelistic work? Oriental religion, notably Hinduism has espoused a syncretistic tolerance oftimes strangling other religious movements in its brotherly embrace. Guided, heretofore, by an attitude of "live and let live," explicit in its contention that tolerance is not a matter only of expedience but of metaphysical principle, Hinduism has grown intolerant about its principle of tolerance. In a report to Secretary General Dag Hammerskjold, A. Krishnaswami, special investigator for the United Nations subcommission on prevention of discrimination and protection of minorities, stated that in India the right of propagation cannot be an absolute right. The issue at present is drawn over the controversial question of "conversion" and "proselytism." It must be said quite candidly that proselyting sects within Christendom have largely fomented the issue. The majority of our Lutheran missionaries have verified the point that sectarian proselytism, often of the most chauvinistic type, has become the bane and disgrace of the Christian witness. There still remains, however, a fundamental Hindu aversion to the concept of conversion. Speaking from the Hindu viewpoint, P. Sanharanarayanan, states that there is a "great resistance to the idea of conversion among Hindus." [10] The dilemma confronting Christianity is that the more it seeks to escape the all-embracing arms of Hinduism, the more it appears to declare itself, from Hindu eyes, to be foreign to the Indian mentality.

Much of the pagan counteraction may be simply the expression of peoples in the infancy of independence when certain excesses of hostile zeal may be expected. But Christianity ought not to be deluded into thinking that it calls only for the patient maintenance of a status-quo. It may very

[9] *Christian Century,* July 21, 1954, p. 872.
[10] *Student World,* Fourth Quarter, 1958, p. 348.

well call for the complete rethinking of the nature, motivation, and strategy of evangelism. Paul Devanandan speaks for
more than India when he states that Christians in India must
demonstrate that the "Christian concern with evangelism
today has no sinister intention and is not the consequence
of an impulse from abroad but of a compulsion from within." [11] True evangelism is surely not a matter of "inducing"
or, worse, "seducing" non-Christians to become converts.
Nor is it the absolute superiority of our religion over all other
religions. That is just what we should not claim! The Gospels
do not speak about Christianity but the "Good News" in
the Word made flesh for the redemption of the world.
Evangelism is not the proclamation of superiority. In the
light of the cross, a stronger case may be made for the proclamation of humility. But, in any event, the Good News will
be broadcast to a paganism in revolt.

Turning closer home to Paganism U.S.A., opposition to
the claims of the Gospel appears more in the form of tacit
indifference. That indifference is born at times of conviction
that religion, like everything else, has its rightful place. But
everything in its own place! Life is carefully compartmented
and each activity of life must be confined to its own compartment. The religion of the Gospel is no exception. Bearers
of the Gospel have been largely willing to follow here the
dictates of the pagan principle. Heightened Christian activity
has scarcely questioned the principle nor sought to attack it.
And as a result the world is spiritually impoverished while
the Gospel lives on in revered isolation. There is no disposition to vote against the Gospel. The Kingdom is a splendid
ideal. By all means, it must be kept as an ideal. It meets with
neither acceptance or rejection, only indifference.

[11] *International Review of Missions,* 1957, p. 266.

Monologue vs. dialogue

The Church has been carrying on a continuous monologue, even though it has been anything but detached from
the world. Theologians have been busily talking to each
other, carefully sharpening and defining their theological
vocabulary, but in a language which the world does not even
understand. A leading Presbyterian layman complained about
the irrelevance of the theological discussions carried on at
the Evanston Assembly of the World Council of Churches.
The voice of the laity was hardly heard. Yet laymen are the
bridge over which the Gospel must pass from the sanctuary
to society. Like the ancient Jews who "localized" God and
thought that he resided only or chiefly in Jerusalem and the
Temple, though pricked by the prophets to think otherwise,
the Christian community has become a fortress walling up
the Gospel instead of a "Gospel Outpost" on the battle-
ground of the world. An introverted society ceases to inform
and transform life around it. It caters only to itself. But the
parish is called to be a mission, an instrument of God's
purpose to redeem the world. Its obligation is to the
neighborhood. The late Edwin E. Aubrey, in examining the
Christian attack on secularism astutely remarks:

"There is always a dilemma in piety . . . It carries with it
the subtle temptation to stay apart from the human
struggle. We try to keep detached from the sin that we
have learned to hate, and in so doing, we fall into other
sins of superciliousness and irresponsibility. Whatever may
have been the risks of the church in the last century becoming too readily identified with the conventional stand-
ards of intellectual and ethical activity, the cure is not to
be found in a retreat from the dangers of the encounter
with secular society. When Jesus spoke of the blind leading

the blind, he was speaking of the ecclesiastical leaders and the pious Pharisees leading the common people. The common people might be blind to the values for which Pharisaism at its best was striving, but the Pharisees had lost their way in a different fashion because they separated themselves from the common life of the time. They sought integrity at the expense of full responsibility for their fellowmen such as some would today find a spurious peace of mind apart from social obligation under God." [12]

Monologue must turn into dialogue. The Church must leave its "insulated charmed circle" and enter into understandable conversation and encounter with the world. The "non-church" movement in Japan, which is beset with obvious dangers (recognized by Japanese churchmen), especially that of the misunderstanding of the meaning of the Church, is a sincere effort, however perilous, to relate the Gospel to the Japanese world and to men who must live in that world. True evangelism never calls mankind into the community of the Church for imprisonment and protracted retreat, but for a missionary calling to be the salt of the earth and the light of the world. As Christians are dispersed from the Church the Word gets to the world.

Every Christian's problem

It is quite easy to assume that though the problem of a pagan world, both in its religiously non-Christian and secularistic forms, may be a paramount concern to specialists within the Church—theologians, missionaries, church leaders and pastors—it is of relatively little moment to the Christian community as a whole. Some have even stated frankly that the parish pastor has no need of concerning himself greatly

[12] Edwin E. Aubrey, *Secularism a Myth,* p. 159.

with the issue. He has much more urgent problems. But is this true? Is the truth not rather that just such unconcern has placed the Gospel in a precarious position of isolation. Let us raise some searching questions.

On one hand one hears the plaintive appeal for world community and oneness, if or no other reason than a basic one of survival. The rapid developments of the twentieth century have produced a world at the same time closer and farther apart. Through language, physical communication, international events, trade and cultural exchanges, mankind has been brought into closer orbit. Yet, not only is there not community, there is large-scale tension and conflict. The deepest need is for spiritual community. Wherein is it to be found? Some see the answer in one of several "universal" faiths. Others plead for a new world syncretistic faith, with or without God. Still others appeal for a commonly agreed-upon humanistic ideal, broadly enough conceived. Is such spiritual community even possible? Are there presently any live options? Can the kingdoms of this world ever become the Kingdom of our God? Does anything less than a universal faith have a chance for survival, not to speak of conquest, in this kind of world? What constitutes a universal faith? Is it man-arrived at, man-created? Can it be humanistically, as over against divinely, conceived?

What bearing, if any, does an understanding of other faiths have upon the knowledge of one's own? What of Max Muller's famous observation, "He who knows only one religion knows none!" Set that over Luther's oft-quoted sentence, "Who knows Christ knows all." What connection, if any, is there between the two? The Gospel is the redemption of all religion as well as the world. But does that redemption proceed apart from knowledge? All peoples have their "father Jacobs" and have drawn water from their fathers' wells for long centuries. Must we not knowingly be aware of that? Is any revival of ancient religions merely a matter of foreign news to American Christians? Is it of any less import than an understanding of the revolutionary developments in the social, economic, and political spheres? Is the problem, after all, not central to our understanding of the life and mission of the Church in the world? D. T. Niles of Ceylon comments: "The question of the relation between Christianity and other religions is a question of permanent theological significance for anyone who seeks to make his preaching effective evangelism." [13]

But, let us be more practical and see the issue at closer range. In a small city outside Nara, Japan, I talked for an afternoon with the "patriarch" of one of Japan's new religions, Tenri-kyo. Though listed for a period under Shinto sects (it claims over two million adherents), it is a synthetic version with a touch of Christian Science added. It, too, was founded by a woman. The important fact to be noted is that this highly publicized faith (acknowledged to be fast growing by central Japanese statistics), equipped with a first-rate public relations office (trained in the U.S.A.), is planning a world-wide mission and already has several hundred missionaries operating in Europe and America. The patriarch himself handed me a free, beautifully printed copy of a lecture he gave at Columbia University in 1954 and reminded me that the American Olympic swimming team competed in the attractive swimming pool (a few years earlier) on their "college compound." Is this an isolated phenomenon?

The World Buddhist Fellowship is already embarked on a world mission strategy. It is estimated that within the next few years the Buddhist missionary force will reach a total of two thousand, a number which exceeds that of Christian

[13] D. T. Niles, *The Preacher's Task*, p. 80.

missionaries at work in Buddhist countries. [14] Buddha has been hailed as the "hope of the world." The complex and often incomprehensible Buddhist scriptures are being carefully worked over by an increasing number of Buddhist scholars (often trained in the West) to be made readable for the Western lay mind. The teachings of Buddha, Mohammed, Ramakrishna, the ancient vedic hymns, the Bhagavad-Gita, the Upanishads, all are blossoming out in bright new paperbacks for passengers at Grand Central Station to scan and purchase. Usually, the contents are edited sufficiently to parallel or harmonize with Christian teaching. At least a segment of the American religious community takes to reading esoteric mystical philosophy, sometimes as a guise of cultural sophistication, to the complete neglect of the Christian scriptures. Students in state and independent universities as well as church colleges, who never got beyond pabulum in Christian instruction are rapidly enrolling in courses in the history of religions, comparative religion and philosophy, introduction to religious thought, etc. Young men fresh from farms will study religion at a university and speak glowingly of the Analects of Confucius, the Four Noble Truths, and the Eightfold Path to home pastors who may still have difficulty even spelling correctly the names of Confucius and Buddha. Theosophical and Self-Realization lectures, given by swamis with fascinating names and titles are attracting an increasing number of city residents, especially middle-aged women, who find a modified yoga not only novel but somewhat exhilarating. The search for Reality and the True Self is intriguing even if it leads them into some placid unreality.

And the "rightness" of Christian missions is not universally endorsed in the churches. Not infrequently is the question raised about the impropriety of invading the religious

[14] *Student World,* Fourth Quarter, 1958, p. 324.

provinces of people who are more religious than we. What right have we to proclaim our religion to a man who has and may be content with his own? What right have we to assume that Christianity solely is the Truth and other time-honored faiths are false? Is not the Oriental precept "each to his own, there are many paths to the top of the mountain," more tolerant and plausible? If his faith is good enough to satisfy him, why intrude with the Gospel? We are all headed for the same place! It may be urgent to witness to Communists or those living in a religious vacuum, but why trouble the others? Missionary activity is a type of aggression. Until Christianity produces such souls of the stature of Vivekenanda, Gandhi, or Radhakrishnan, there is little justification for extensive evangelism.

Now students and church members are either asking these questions outright or else are thinking them. If you doubt that, survey your youth and young adult groups. At times they provide their own quick answers to these questions. The universality of the Gospel is a very local problem. And the problem must be dealt with intelligently by pastors.

The problem of a secularistically pagan world in our midst is no less a matter of concern for all. Every parish is aware of the "good, moral, faithful, but unbelieving husband." C. S. Lewis's "Christian Miss Bates" with her unkind tongue, and the "unbelieving Dick Firkin" with his placid temperament are known to us all. And what of that large segment of secular America, professors, doctors, scientists, businessmen, lawyers, and laborers, who consciously remain outside the Christian community, unresponsive to the Gospel, yet continue to maintain positions of honor, prestige, and usefulness to society? There is no hostility there, just religious immunity. Are they beyond the necessity for salvation? What can redemption mean for them? How can they be reached?

2

CULTURED DESPISERS

Funeral directors are rarely theologians but they occasionally drop comments which preachers may grab hold of and convert into homiletical grist. The owner of the Simpson Funeral Home was deploring the large scale unconcern of many of his patrons for religion and the Church. He was commenting specifically upon a recent funeral where the husband was making the necessary arrangements for a "nice funeral" for his wife. Mr. Simpson asked the man the name of the preacher. The husband paused awkwardly for a second and then in unabashed ignorance replied: "Preacher? Do you need one?" "Not really," said Simpson, "but all the best funerals do!" "All right, can you get me a Protestant then?" queried the bereaved. "Yes, but it will cost you ten dollars for his services." "Ten dollars, just for the preacher?" And with that he hit the ceiling! Mr. Simpson was silently indignant at the man's impropriety and lack of a sense of religious fitness. To think that onyone would prepare for the funeral of a loved one without the ministrations of a church. What Simpson failed to see was the perfect consistency, and if I may add, the complete propriety of the man's action. No religion or preacher was necessary during her life. Why at her death?

The incident may be somewhat abnormal but by no means uncommon. Most people are likely, at least in death, to turn to some religion for solace. As a matter of fact, though two-thirds of the population in America is somewhere other than at worship on Sunday morning, there is more religious activity than in any period in our national history. And it must be repeated that much of the activity is genuine. Religion today is given a wide opening. But religious stirring is one thing, religious relevancy another. Religiosity and secularism pace each other down the street. Never has there been a greater dichotomy of faith and life than in modern society. On the one hand, an insatiable religious appetite and on the other an uncontrollable propensity to worship at secular altars. Where men place their offerings and center their primary interests is where their real religion is to be found. Is God, God; or is he a god?

The great defection

It must be quite evident that Dietrich Bonhoeffer's comment in the *Ecumenical Review* is dead on center: "Everything gets along without God and just as well as before. As in the scientific field, so in the domain of general human affairs, what we call "God" is being more and more edged out of life, losing more and more ground." [1] As long ago as the Jerusalem Conference of the International Missionary Council (1928), the Quaker Rufus Jones warned the Christian world that the greatest rival of the Gospel is not Buddhism or Islam or any of the other great faiths but secularism. And, if Jones were living now, he would add the note that the same secularistic spirit is the chief contemporary rival of those religions. Were it not for the fact that we religiously-minded people have an almost incurable tendency to look on the bright side of things we might see this "creeping totalitarian religion" (David Roberts) for the menace it is. God is no longer, if ever he were, the working hypothesis of our world. "Modern life," writes Dr. Harry Emerson Fosdick, "is shot through and through with a gross debasing paganism (secu-

[1] *Ecumenical Review*, January, 1952, p. 135.

larism)," until not only is the Reality of God himself distant to man, but the very "profundities in man are depreciated, defamed and denied." [2]

So paramount in human experience are the natural, the material, and the solely human, that God and the whole realm of spiritual reality are deemed non-essential for the conduct of life and thought. Content with the prevailing gods, the touchstone of idolatry, contemporary society has out-moloched the ancients. We have not altogether done away with God. We have no stomach for that. Caution, religious nostalgia and indecision have prevented it. We have simply chosen to organize our private lives, our decisions, and daily activities as if God were not around, or as if he did not mind or perchance did not know. As Professor Paul Tillich would say, we fix our prime attention upon and attach our deepest loyalties to our private concerns and act as if they were the one ultimate concern. Whether it is our work, or pleasure, or money, or family, or nation, all of which deserve a rightful place, they become "absolutized relativities." Like Martha, we become absolutely concerned about a variety of things and only relatively concerned about the One Thing needful. [3] If idolatry has been a basic and perennial problem of religion, it is the paramount one now. Quite frankly we have put something less than God in the place belonging only to God. For all our religiosity, we are nonetheless a tragically Godless people. How far wrong was Nietzsche when he wrote about the contemptible struggle for wealth in the Western world and spoke of the Christian God as dead?

More and more areas are being lifted out of God's domain and Screwtape is now busily plotting his master strategy of segregating religion itself from the Gospel. Samuel Butler's

[2] H. E. Fosdick, *Riverside Sermons*, p. 48.
[3] Paul Tillich, *The New Being*, pp. 152-160.

words have a peculiarly modern relevance: "There are all too many folk of whom it might be said that they would be equally horrified at hearing Christianity doubted or at seeing it practiced." [4] Notwithstanding glowing statistics, it is a moot question to ask how many Christians have added a truly Christian orientation to their lives. Secularism has drawn a mighty trump and gone religious with a vengeance. Or rather, modern man has become a frank and unashamed secularist devotee. He has not cashed in the religious symbols. He has simply adapted them to a secular culture. Secularism dominates the American scene. Smile or shudder as we will at the husband making arrangements for his wife's funeral, there is a tragic reality and consistency in his comments.

Secularism is hard to pin down. It has no avowed creed or substance. It has issued no manifestoes. It is organized with no church or association. No one *belongs* to secularism. One cannot speak of it as militant for it pervades rather than marches. It is hard to define for it takes many forms. At best it can only be described. Herberg refers to it as "thinking and living in terms of a framework of reality and value remote from the religious beliefs simultaneously professed." [5] The implication is that a person may be a professed Christian and an unprofessed secularist at the same time. Much as a Japanese can be simultaneously a Buddhist, Shintoist—and secularist—and usually is. Indeed this pluralistic character to one's loyalties is the main trademark of secularism. It means the absence of conflict and the dominance of fragmentation. Each compartment of life enjoys its own autonomy and they remain unjoined and mutually exclusive. The question of an absolute autonomy is not raised. Religion, politics and aesthetics maintain their own criteria of authority and value and they need never clash.

[4] W. Norman Pittenger, *Christ in the Haunted Wood*, p. 168.
[5] Will Herberg, *Protestant-Catholic-Jew*, p. 14.

Though the secularistic viewpoint may not formally repudiate God—it usually does not much care one way or the other—it does tend to consider him so irrelevant that for all practical purposes God does not exist.[6] He is simply crowded out. If atheistic, secularism is practical rather than theoretical atheism. The nineteenth and early twentieth centuries may have seen the band of aggressive agnostics, free-thinkers, and organized atheists and the Clarence Darrows, who declared open war on the churches and religion, but America in the 1950's can scarcely be said to sport a hostile movement of irreligion. [7] On the contrary, secularism is polite. It does not bother to repudiate, it overlooks and so squeezes out religion. It becomes so absorbed in things, often worthwhile things, that the insidiousness of its threat is not easily recognized.

Christianity has not always been sympathetic to the good secularism has accomplished, much of which may be a by-product of Christianity itself. [8] The intense preoccupation with the things of this world, often but not always, to the disregard of God and His Kingdom, has produced a sizeable package of blessings in health, education, welfare, cultural appreciations and social improvements. On the credit side, secularism has accomplished much good in the world though it has borrowed heavily from the faith of the fathers. So heavily in fact that it is difficult to distinguish between which fruit is secular and which sacred.

Still, secularism lifts God from the center of life, crowds him out to the edge, and by so doing isolates its own goods from the love, worship and service of him who is man's Supreme Good. The City of Man supplants the City of God. Pride in man's self-sufficiency is Lord. And the Gospel judges it as unpardonable. The seed sown among thorns, in Jesus'

[6] Georgia Harkness, *The Modern Rival of Christian Faith,* p. 16.
[7] Herberg, *op. cit.,* p. 59f.
[8] Howard Lowry, *The Mind's Adventure,* p. 22.

parable, is an excellent description of the danger of the secularistic life. The cares, riches, and pleasures, even the positive
goods of this life may threaten to choke out spiritual religion.
Secularism, no organized movement of a sinister and
malicious nature but a casual growth, is the most subtle
despiser of the Gospel.

This secularistic spirit is quite extensive and penetrating
in its reach. The much-heralded spiritual revival of today has
done little to reverse the essentially secular standard of
values or pattern of behaviour. Take the matter of choosing
one's profession. See how quickly discussion turns upon the
financial possibilities of this or that type of position. Primary
questions gather about the quality of the position, the prom-
ise it holds and the opportunities for advancement—the more
rapid, the better. Not that these matters should be of no
consequence or concern or that they are not of legitimate
interest for the inquirer. But, sadly enough, vocational guidance has lost what has been referred to as its "cosmic setting."
The concept of "vocation" has given place to the more important discussion and discovery of one's particular tastes,
qualifications and prevailing needs, all of which are quite
relevant but which quickly overshadow, if not altogether displace, the important criterion of ultimate meaning and true
personal fulfillment. Is the sacredness of a calling reserved
only for religious occupations? Is there no divine perspective
in secular occupations?

Or take marriage. Was not Pittenger's woman, who said of
her marriage, "though it was perfectly happy, it lacked a
cosmic setting and was therefore all wrong," laying hold of a
sound principle often ignored in the contemporary world?
Marriage is not so much a holy estate as a happy or unhappy
arrangement, which, though it may continue successfully,
never achieves its deepest expression and at the worst, in
moments of crisis, finds no point of divine reference from

which it may rediscover its charter and be saved from dissolution. The acids of secularistic modernity have eaten away at the heart of the marriage vows.

Follow secularism into a quite different avenue. Mass media of communication are preparing more than we are ready to admit the seedbed for the intellectual and moral judgments of our generation and the next. "We live more and more in an atmosphere of passive acceptance in which asking questions is becoming a sign of eccentricity; and we are hardly aware of the part played by our mass media in creating this sluggish mood." [9] A highly stylized and accomplished art of advertising has developed, posing all sorts of ethical questions. By the use of mass media, skilled advertising has manipulated man into the "mass man" and contributed greatly to his depersonalization and incidentally bastardized the various media of communication. Manufacturers, aided by Motivation Research, have not hesitated to exploit human frailties and pander to human weaknesses.

The editor of the *Hartford Courant,* America's oldest newspaper, recently pointed out that if the press is to avoid writing its own obituary it must "rethink its mission in today's world and revive the underlying moral purpose of journalism." At the risk of the criticism of subjective reporting, the press must rise above the slavish recapping of events and learn "reporting in depth . . . to go beyond the superficial and attributable opinions into underlying causes and meanings." [10]

How extensive have been the secularistic inroads into the arts? Three obvious characteristics of much of contemporary literature are fragmentation, debasement and despair. Fragmentation—what the poet Archibald MacLeish once called "this fracture at the center of our civilization"—because in our modern mania for analysis and specialization without

[9] Gilbert Seldes, *The Great Audience,* p. 3.
[10] *Saturday Review*, April 25, 1959.

the discovery of purposive synthesis, there has been found no solid center of meaning. To be sure there are first-rate writers—men like T. S. Eliot and W. H. Auden who through their Christianly-oriented writing have discovered the sense of wholeness and meaning. Others like Somerset Maugham, William Faulkner, Boris Pasternak and Wyndham Lewis, to mention a few, have understood the lostness of our time and have exposed the tragic predicament of modern man. More than that, they have reflected a "groping for salvation" (a word they would not use).[11] But the fact remains that many modern writers see a man as an unrelated fragment. He is a tragic island unto himself. "If man is part of a whole thing, he is more than himself; he is meaningful and important. If he is only a random collection of atoms accidentally coming together, without relationship to a whole, he is invalid and without meaning. It is as simple and as clear as that. If man is a part of the whole then we define him in terms of a whole; if not, he is an eternally irrelevant fragment."[12] In a time when we ought to be in the most favorable position to understand a great deal of the nature of man through the knowledge provided by psychology, anthropology and sociology, we have succeeded only in obscuring rather than clarifying our idea of man. Man has become more problematic to himself than in any previous period and the confusion is startlingly vivid in much of contemporary literature.[13] Bereft of divine presuppositions of faith, many writers are left with the infractuous world of introspection with no clear answer to the fundamental question, "What is man?"

With fragmentation have come debasement and despair.

[11] I am indebted to a good friend and keen observer for this point, Dr. Russell S. Stroup of Washington, D.C.

[12] Calvin D. Linton, "The Crisis in Modern Literature," a lecture delivered at the Church of the Reformation, Washington, D.C. in the series, *"The Crisis in Modern Culture."*

[13] Malcolm Cowley, "Ten Authors in Pursuit of One Subject," *Horizon*, March, 1959, Vol. I, No. 4, pp. 14-17; 117-119.

Having lost the high concept of man, secularized culture has produced a type of literature that often revels in a repellent and loathsomely deformed view of the human self unmoored from its divine source. And all of it in a seeming regard of self and in the name of "realism." Playwright Tennessee Williams at times almost appears to have exchanged his literary talents for the credentials of a clinical pathologist. His ribald writing on perverted human conduct reads more like a confidential session with the psychiatrist than a legitimate description from the pen of a literary artist. That depraved human nature is like that is not the issue. And human experience of whatever character is fitting subject matter for the writer. But literature is one thing, clinical reports another.

The abundant literature of despair and meaninglessness hits a low in the near schizophrenic, nihilistic productions of the "beat writers" who inhabit the North Beach area of San Francisco and the Lower East Side of New York. Jack Kerouac, the prototype of these literary bohemians, in such works as *On the Road, The Subterraneans, Playboy,* and *The Dharma Bums* (playing upon a Buddhist theme), finds the essential tragedy of modern life to lie in emptiness. Like the hero Ray Smith searching for Reality (Dharma) in the *Dharma Bums,* and the frantic young people of *On the Road* searching wildly for "something" more satisfying than comfortable security, "beat" philosophy and literature concludes that the "something" is the idea that nothing really matters. The characters who speed now, jazz now, mope now, and do most anything across the pages are like the cold shadows that walk in Eliot's *Waste Land.* The hollow men of a godless era know tragically the meaning of the collect "without whom (God) nothing is strong, nothing is holy." And the nothingness adds up to distortion and despair. To be aware of the lost state of man and to be responsibly concerned about it is to set one foot at least upon the road back; not to be aware of it or to be aware but resigned is to plunge deeper into the spiritual darkness of this generation. Much of modern literature is but a dramatic and sometimes sordid description of lostness rather than a search for meaning and redemption.

A similar mood prevails in much of modern drama and art. Plays too often either totter between pointlessness or hopelessness. To argue that this is the human raw material which a fractured world offers the dramatist is only partly the truth. Also offered, by virtue of the tragic human predicament, is the very environment out of which great plays may be born. What is really lacking is depth of perception and commitment. This could very well become the great age of drama, if only otherwise gifted playwrights were to emerge from spiritual immaturity to deal with the human situation from the vantage point of knowledge about the true nature of man. Lesser dramatists become mired solely in the avalanche of feelings and sheer futility. Great writers are able to deal with the human tragedy without resigning, and more importantly, to find spiritual significance. The absence or irrelevancy of the supernatural is the key to the failure. The great playwrights of the Greek and Elizabethan theatre could tackle the desperate conflicts between man, the world and God, the tragic experiences of guilt, suffering, death, and despair, and come out with meaning. In a secularistic age, the curtain falls on meaninglessness.

Much of the contemporary art simply reflects the same spiritual sickness and lack of spiritual resources in the modern artist himself. The late director of the Metropolitan Museum of Art, writing in the *Saturday Evening Post,* appealed for a return to reality, meaning and a cosmic sense in art: " (Man) has become, indeed, the arbiter of his own fate, but he has not yet learned that the cosmic is distinguished from the comic by only a single consonant . . . Meaning it (art) must have . . . Despair appears to be perhaps the most familiar trademark of the contemporary artist . . . he is creating in a vacuum . . . Revelation of the universe is not to be had merely for the asking. It requires humility and faith—faith in a divine order more considerable than the petty emotional experiences of man himself. To create, a man must give himself; and if he gives himself, he must believe. Then, and only then, will his work shine with the contentment of the archaic smile." [14]

A recently retired national educator has stated that the crises in modern education is in great measure due to a lack of the sense of history and the continuing dedication of human minds to trivialities. Education has been largely characterized by the failure to address itself to fundamental questions. It has been satisfied to slide along the horizontal line of broadened information without tackling the vertical line of meaning. Largely through an epidemic of naturalistic-humanistic philosophy, (not altogether without significant blessings) begun by John Dewey and carried on by the teachers colleges under his influential thought, American public education espoused a kind of popular religion, a democratic faith, which avoided the pitfalls of sectarian teaching (rightly so) but which in turn created its own "non-sectarian" creed formalized in a statement of abstract "moral and spiritual values." A synthetic deity, *god-in-general* substituted for *any-god-in-particular* because it was presumably acceptable to all religious traditions.[15] There is no hostile secularity there. Indeed, thoughtful and religiously-committed educators are not satisfied with an educational philosophy that tears away values from their religious roots and tries to impart them in vague detachment. Isolated, these value-fruits of the

[14] Frances H. Taylor, "Art and Human Dignity," *Saturday Evening Post,* May 17, 1958.
[15] *Christianity Today,* May 12, 1958.

biblical Christian (not Judeo-Christian) tradition tend to get watered down into an undefined faith equally as sectarian as any it supplants. It is a short step that points to full-scale divorce.

Now, though the secularistic spirit, sharply focused upon all the significant places of our western culture (in vocations, marriage, the arts, education, etc.) results in inevitable moods of fragmentation, despair and irrelevance which are the results of every concern and activity divorced from their ultimate reference in God, the very predicament created provides the framework for a redemptive solution. Christianity has its chance. But Osborn offers a caution: "The fundamental test of a true spiritual revival in the contemporary world is not the mere flourishing of institutional religion or even the increase of personal piety; it is the degree to which there may be regained for a transcendant faith the throne of decision which has been usurped by autonomous secular concerns." [16] America cannot just go to church and pray. Convictions cannot just be staunchly maintained. They must have direct bearing upon those decisions that determine events in society. The horizontal lines of concern in our day must regain their attachment to the vertical "dimension of depth." Extensive scrutiny and repairs must first be made in the house of the Lord.

Secularized Christianity

It is instinctive with us preachers to beleaguer secularism as if it were a devilish menace which threatened only from without. Churches and Christians are both highly secularized. Not only has secularism gained extensive footholds within the folds of organized Christianity, but the pervasiveness of its power may be largely attributable to a fundamental weak-

[16] Ronald E. Osborn, *The Spirit of American Christianity*, p. 204.

ness and loss of intelligible communication in Christianity. "The Church's secularization," writes Kraemer, "is even more serious than the world's, because one is largely blinded to it by the "holy" or 'sacral' cloak in which everything is disguised." [17] The renascence of religion is only a temporary smokescreen hiding the rampancy of secularism, not a contradiction to it.

Secularization within Christianity takes many and diverse turns. One form of it appears in a kind of theological and biblical isolationism in which the language from the pulpit sounds more like the "ancient language of Canaan" than the language which men speak in the heavy traffic of their daily lives. Doctrinal and biblical preaching may be quite correct but fall like "stones rather than bread" upon worshippers who desire desperately to relate the Good News to their own unhappy situations. The Evanston Assembly of the World Council of Churches (1954) called forth the most able theological minds of our time to formulate with theological correctness the message of "Christ the Hope of the World." Yet one can hardly blame the lay community for the failure to see, in what sense, for them, he is the hope of the world. "Undiluted, unrealized and realized eschatology" is hardly the language for the man on Main Street, not to mention the possibility of irresponsibility and irrelevance of the neo-orthodox eschatology itself. How does all that relate to the pressing responsibilities of modern living? That the Gospel itself is terribly relevant to the human situation, and the only real hope for it, is not to say that all theological formulations of the Gospel are! Some are operating hopelessly in a theological ghetto. Meanwhile, the Gospel remains out of circulation in the world while the Church nourishes its own specialized brand of "religious secularism."

Another expression of secularized Christianity lies in a

[17] Kraemer, *Communication of the Christian Faith*, p. 84.

type of eviscerated Gospel—pernicious Gospel anemia—so
ably described by Martin Marty in his articles in 1958, in
the *Christian Century*. The Church itself has often succeeded
in rendering the Gospel barren. It is as if the Gospel had
been plunged into some sterilizing fluid so that any particle
of it that might possibly startle, condemn or mystify people
were deadened. Once made harmless, the Gospel became
insipid, prudent, and acceptable. And then men spew it
forth. Speaking of this devitalized Gospel proclaimed from
American pulpits, Sittler says: "The cult of acceptance is
polite. Polite as hell. It has its own grace; the graciousness
of no expectation; the suavity of emptiness; the courtesy of
non-significance." [18] The probing Gospel with the cutting
edge is exchanged for a feathery Gospel which tickles our
religious fancy and brushes aside some of our more obvious
faults but does not begin to stand us up to full judgment.
D. T. Niles of Ceylon once remarked that he had never seen
a purer form of Vedanta than in the present version of
religion in America. It is everything to everybody. How
little like evangelical Christianity the pro-religious atmosphere of America sometimes really is! The important thing
seems to be not the character of one's religion but simply that
he be in some sense religious. The Gospel in that atmosphere
is hardly to be considered a serious option.

In the eviscerated Gospel, God exists primarily to be used;
running assorted human errands, managing the "peace of
mind and prosperity of pocket" cults, keeping up batting
averages for "religious outfielders" (never mind the opposing
pitchers' earned run averages), answering the "telephone
dial-a-prayer service," invocating miscellaneous conventions
and so on. If not the principal, he is one of the means to
selfish human ends. God is exploited as the "miracle product
to solve all ills." The High and Holy One has been pulled

---

[18] The author cannot locate the quotation.

down and dragged into the market places of the world not to redeem those market places but to be made marketable for human purposes. In place of the retreat from Christianity into irreligion comes the invasion of irreligion into Christianity. As Chad Walsh says: "God becomes an agent, an instrument for obtaining happiness, security, and the other modern beatitudes. We can get the by-products of religion directly, without first loving God and our neighbor." [19]

In the eviscerated Gospel, evangelism promotes Christ like cereal, exchanges the offense of the cross for symbols of success and evaluates effectiveness after the manner of the Hooper ratings. One is reminded of the criticism by Dick Sheppard of that fatuous confidence that once the necessary ecclesiastical reforms have been brought about, masses of people will crowd the churches: "If the Churches were to become out-and out Christian, and if all their ministers were to prophesy—that is, to speak the flaming word of God in the hearing of the people—it is more than likely that places of worship would be emptier than they are today." [20] Modern evangelism, in both motive and techniques, runs a constant danger of exploiting men for Christ after the fashion of the world, instead of winning them in the manner of the Gospel. While the Orient pursues the fallacy of preaching world renunciation as good religion, the West preaches success as the criterion of truth in religion as everywhere else. Tillich expressed the idea that religion may die of a surfeit of its own excesses and successes. The Church needs to search itself in its evangelistic enthusiasm. Why is it interested in the unchurched? For the sake of publishable gains? To keep pace with competitors? To support expanding budgets? Is evangelism a subterfuge or the constraint of divine love and the inward compulsion of a thankful heart?

[19] *Saturday Review,* December 6, 1958.
[20] *The Best of Dick Sheppard,* Edited by H. E. Luccock, p. 48.

In the eviscerated Gospel, the Church either takes on a gray-flanneled conformity to the world it is intended to reform or else it locks itself up into something called the "purely religious." In either case it loses its sense of mission and the Gospel operates in a vacuum. As a "purely religious" concern the Church huddles into a ghetto of its own making and there is a strong biblical judgment upon that. God himself was sufficiently concerned about the world to incarnate his word into it for the purpose of redeeming it. The late William Temple once observed that it is a mistake to suppose that God is only or even chiefly concerned with religion. His real concern is for the world and any church that continues talking too long to itself becomes peculiar. And not peculiarly Christian! The inevitable consequence of becoming "purely religious," leaving more and more of the world out of the concern of the Church, is to lift God out of the world. God becomes definitely optional as he now largely is. As Bishop Bayne puts it: "The Church that has accepted the dogma of the optional God is a Church that has abdicated its mission to human society; it has no mission; it has only a seat in the secular train, at clergy rates, which apply only to the slower trains." [21] The Gospel is devitalized and the Church secularized.

But there is an equal temptation in the other direction—namely to become a comfortably conformed Church. Churches are now becoming as "well-adjusted" to the world as their people are. It may very well be that it is not the tragedy and confusion of the times that is turning people to the Church, but the discovery that they don't have to be peculiar to belong. The Bible may once have spoken about "God's peculiar people" but the differentiation between church membership and club membership is no longer so obvious. Personality integration has replaced character,

[21] Stephen F. Bayne, *The Optional God,* p. 23.

morale takes precedence over morality, and an easy tolerance outranks indignation. "Be not conformed to this world" offers no real problem. The Church has exchanged its conscience for a mirror. The biting words of Dick Sheppard are a jolt to us all: "I suggest that it is high time that we all —not excluding parsons—should determine whether we desire and would support a Church that would risk and give its life as its Lord did, rather than compromise the will of God, or whether we should prefer some mild and manageable version of religion that would be willing to make us comfortable and call our pagan emotions by gentle names." [22]

The moral and social problem of racial relations in America is, among other things, a glaring example of the secularization of the Church. With full recognition of the need for a wise Christian strategy as well as a faithfulness to Christian principle, it must nevertheless be confessed that the Church of Christ has not only conformed to the world but to a real degree lagged behind it. Paradoxically, the Gospel which has fathered much of the idealism for human understanding and equality has met up with its sharpest obstacle in the spiritual community created to proclaim it. But not altogether so. Churches in convention (where it is easiest to do so) have at times been verbally prophetic. A few churches in the secular community, where it is hardest, have been courageously prophetic. But generally, the Church is found in the rearguard, not the vanguard, of Christian social action. The likelihood is that the church will proceed at the world's pace not at the gait of the Gospel.

Secularism as judge and servant

We have tried to describe, not define, this cultured despiser of Christianity and the extensiveness of its inroads

[22] *The Best of Dick Sheppard*, p. 139.

into modern culture. It is the pagan god of the Western world, quite content to have man's theoretical worship directed to the True God so long as his practical worship is offered at secular altars. The most subtle thrust of secularism has been into the very camp of Christianity and the Church. "If you can't lick them, join them" has been its strategy. And it has obviously paid off.

Now we must see secularism for what it really is. There is much truth in the late Professor Aubrey's claim that "secularism is a myth." That is, the secularism the Church has been declaiming often is only an imaginary entity which becomes little more than a convenient whipping post for all sorts of things. Perhaps it is not a god so much as a fallen angel. As the latter term suggests, a mixture of good and bad; a legitimate and worthwhile concern, nobly sired, but which has fallen from grace and set up its own cathedrals. The result is idolatry. Secularism has delivered its blessings and at the same time has become an instrument of judgment. As Tillich observes, Protestantism which helped to spawn secularism is in need of that secularism to guard itself from an ever-threatening religious and ecclesiastical infallibility and complacency which may prevent its true realization. [23] "The more that Protestantism is able and willing to accept secular criticism of itself, the more it acquires the right and power to criticize secularism." [24]

Like the ancient Assyrians who were obliquely in the service of the Divine Wrath against the unfaithful and impious Israel, secularism has served as a divine shock treatment to stir the Church, even when as an " 'ism" the secular world itself is judged. The full roots of secularism are too complex to be traced superficially in such a brief study. One must travel back, perhaps as far as the late period of the

[23] Paul Tillich, *The Protestant Era*, pp. 213-221.
[24] *Ibid.* p. 219.

early church, to understand medieval conflict of the Church with the world, the extravagances of the Renaissance and the whole scientific, industrial and social revolution of the modern era. But healthy criticism must, nevertheless, be leveled at organized Christianity itself.

In its thoughtless polemic against the secular world, its negative institutional reaction to large scale developments in society, which paradoxically its Gospel message largely generated, and in its tendency to identify itself with particular status-quos, the Church has not only lost face and prestige but character. May not much of the practical (there is very little theoretical) atheism of our time be a noble protest against an irrelevant and degrading form of Christianity? May not Marxism have attained such a following because of the failure of official Christianity to become the advocate of down trodden man and the success of communism be attributable to religion's support of an intolerable status quo?[25] Which Christ has been rejected both by communism and non-Christian faiths? The Christ of the Gospel or an idolistic and institutional caricature?

A lot of the airy utopianism of self-styled Christian optimists has been quickly and rightly dismissed as "mere sentimentality" by secular minds. In how many breezy sermons have we preachers peeled off broad and easy solutions and with pontifical confidence—to what are actually very complex problems! "To engage the intelligence of our time, evangelism will have to employ an intellectually honest theology—a theology which humbly confesses its past sins of blindness to truths delivered by science or realistic secular thought, yet which boldly confronts false secular dogmas with those of biblical faith."[26]

The Church, for example, has rightly lamented the loss

[25] Hendrik Kraemer, *Ecumenical Review*, Vol. IX, p. 128.
[26] *Ecumenical Study Report for the Evanston Assembly*.

in society of the sense of vocation and is shocked by the modern obsession with a professionalism and successism which have little regard for the motive of unselfish service. Economic materialism has produced a mad scramble to get to the top and "right early." It is without doubt one of the great tragedies of our time. Yet how much of it may be due to the Church itself which has often "talked big" about the Christian conception of vocation but has failed miserably to encourage or help work out in concrete ways a practical *modus vivendi* for a Christian in business, a doctor, lawyer, teacher, laborer. One of the most hopeful developments in the contemporary strategy of evangelism is the Christian engagement with the professions. Men who have thus far found their prime fellowship and *raison d'etre* in labor unions, professional societies, service organizations and suburban country clubs (the modern principalities and powers) may yet discover in the fellowship of the Holy Spirit the nature of their true being and the eternal significance of their occupation. [27]

Secularism may turn out to be a vast cathartic movement, one of the mysterious though ironic ways God uses to summon the Church back to its true nature and mission, namely that of proclaiming, but more likely demonstrating, the Lordship of Christ and his Kingdom over all of life. If so, secularism may yet be transmitted into a blessing. If on the one hand, the Church can be drawn out of its "charmed insular" position to be intelligently concerned about the world, and if, on the other hand, in the place of just comfortably mirroring the world, it can with true Christian non-conformity claim, not condemn, the world for the Gospel, then secularism may

[27] Two excellent publications are rewarding reading at this point: E. R. Wickham, *The Church and the People in an Industrial City,* and the pamphlet, *Signs of Renewal, Life of the Lay Institutes in Europe,* Department of the Laity, World Council of Churches.

not be considered wholly a spiritual liability. But the Church must move with all seriousness and wisdom.

A Christian approach

The Church must acknowledge quickly the positive gains made by a secularistic society largely without benefit of the Church and the direct activity of the Gospel. Only in a slim tangential sense can it be claimed that the Church had much to do with many of the humanitarian achievements of this generation. The improvement in the status of the laboring classes, for example, and the progress made in securing greater racial equality have not been by the grace of organized Christianity. Indeed, the Church has been either listed among the obstacles to such advancement, or thought of as a "Johnny come lately." The gains have come largely through pressure movements, themselves a mixture of good and bad, and a thoroughly secularistic philosophy. Again, in the field of education, though the Church has been quite critical of secular higher education and often has hurled at it the deadly epithet "godless"— perhaps as much for the sake of its own defense and advantage (it is one way of gathering financial support)—it has not always been appreciative or even aware of the gains that have been made in the universities. Aubrey seems to me to have, at least in part, a justifiable resentment of that critical attitude of the Church on the three grounds he lists: (1) The Church has not mastered the art of education enough to do a significant job in its own domain and is therefore scarcely fitted to instruct the universities in the task; (2) suspicion that the Church is masking under the guise of a concern for Christian values its uneasiness about critical study of religious ideas in the classrooms in philosophy, sociology, history, or biology; (3) church critics are not studying carefully the steps which colleges and universities are taking to correct abuses in the pursuit of truth, which is their special responsibility. [28]

But acknowledgement and gratitude for the gains of a secular world is only preliminary. Unless it leads to wholesome, self-criticism, self-purgation and a new self-discovery in the church it has little value. The heart of the Christian approach to the problem of secularization is the recovery of the true meaning and mission of the Church. Not in theological discussion but in the actual reality of the parish. Not in world and national ecclesiastical conventions but through local congregations where the real encounters of the Gospel with the world take place.

My friend, Bishop Angus Dun, of the Washington Diocese of the Episcopal Church, stated modestly several years ago at a luncheon conversation that it was comparatively easy for a bishop to make a bold pronouncement from his see on a controversial social issue where the Gospel was directly involved; it was quite another and more difficult matter for a parish pastor to speak to his immediate parishioners on the issue. His life is intimately involved in theirs and they pay his salary. The point may be taken a step further. It still is more difficult for the parishioner himself to relate this same Gospel at the center of the issue where he daily finds himself. Yet there is the locus of the encounter.

In all three marks of the Church, kerygma, diakonia, and koinonia, *at the local level,* there must be revaluation and action. It may call for quite radical departures. In proclamation, not just from the pulpit, there must be actual discourse and encounter with the world, through Christian laymen who are in the world. That calls for imagination and realistic communication from clergy and laity. In service (diakonia) the Church must be prepared to lay its Christian conviction

[28] Aubrey, *op. cit.,* p. 176.

"on the line," identify itself fully, as a servant, with the sufferings, fears, temptations, and aspirations of men, though always guided not by what the world desires but by what the Gospel claims. In fellowship (koinonia) the Church must become far more than a "spiritualized club" which takes most of its cues largely from social organisms. It must actually be in its structure, program and life (we are speaking still of the local congregation) the body of Christ, bent on nurturing the souls who are already within it as well as those who may be drawn into this realized community of God, and then dispersing them as redeemed, committed disciples into the world. All this calls for an extensive review of the entire program of evangelism.

The church is the fellowship of believers, committed and less-committed to Christ, people at various levels of spiritual attainment. Some understand the language of the Church, some do not. Some are ready for higher steps of commitment and responsibility, some are not.

Undoubtedly, part of the explanation for Billy Graham's appeal is that many come to the revival to take the first step in discipleship and feel themselves unready for the Church. The truth may be that because the Church in its evangelism presupposes a level of attainment to which some have not yet risen, the Church itself may be the unready one.

High among considerations, the Church in its approach to the secularistically oriented world, both in its midst and outside it, must declare a relevant and understandable Gospel. It must truly open up the Scriptures to its hearers. The Bible is at once the most sacred and irrelevant body of literature in the modern world. Like the sacred cow of India it is worshipped even when it is useless. The greatest instrument of God's word has become a closed and sealed book to the majority of the laity. "Though they have a vague attitude of reverence for the book, they don't quite know what to do with it." [29] Because its language seems so far removed from their contemporary ways of thinking as well as their immediate problems, it remains a book for the religious specialist. The Church has a herculean assignment of translating it into contemporary thought forms. It must be done if the faith once delivered to the saints is to be made applicable to the modern communion of saints. Continued failure at this point only drives the world farther away from the redeeming Gospel.

The most direct and meaningful approach of the Church to a world secularistically isolated from the Gospel is through the ministrations of a committed lay apostolate. How else does the Word get to the world except through the laity? And the chief business of the minister is to train the laity to communicate it. Clearly the most prophetic and far-reaching work of the Church in recent years comprises the experiments in lay witnessing carried on through lay institutes, extensively throughout Europe and to a lesser extent in selected American religious communities. Into industry, labor, the professions, and government, the Gospel must be carried by the lay dispersion. This is not easily accomplished and demands much study and preparation. But if the secular world is to be won to the Lordship of Christ, a way must be found. Men may never be drawn into the institutional church as we know it, but they may be lifted up, in some sense, into the Church outside the Church. Perhaps only in that way, and to that degree, will the Gospel ever encounter a world tragically separated from God.

The establishment of a coffee house in downtown Washington, D. C. by a small congregation may strike a traditionally-oriented Church as a rather bizarre and bohemian form of evangelism, unbefitting a fellowship of Christ. But if through such a structure the Gospel can be communicated

[29] Kraemer, *Communication of the Christian Faith,* p. 93.

to those who would never enter the Church (never mind their reasons!) who will say that the method is invalid? Said the pastor of the congregation to a reporter, "The coffee house would serve as a conversational center, a place for serious talk where non-religious persons can ask religious questions and get answers." [80] To be sure there is the risk that the secular man may get inadequate or wrong answers or may draw the conclusion, in true intellectual fashion, that being religious is synonymous with being religiously conversant (everybody knows religion is a popular topic); but the risk is not half as great as a damning silence where no opportunity is offered even for the asking of questions. The Gospel has no chance at all where there is no meeting. Hosts of people sought out Jesus even as they seek out the Church. But Jesus also said to a Zacchaeus, " . . . I must stay at your house today." (Luke 19:5). If the factory worker will not come to the Church, then the Church must find some way of meeting him where he is. He already may have concluded that the Church is interested in him only as a member, not as a factory worker.

In this encounter of the Gospel with secularism we may come to learn the deeper meaning of the Incarnation of Christ. The secular involvement of Christianity or the influence of the secular in Christianity is not an unmitigated evil. Contrary to its being a "sad deficiency" it may be a great opportunity. Is not the incarnation, after all, God's own personal involvement in the plight of the world? In the only way in which the world could know what was in the mind of God, his word was made flesh and dwelt among men, in the world where they were, in the world where they were to be redeemed. Unlike the oriental conception in which Godhead was incarnated to deliver men out of the

[80] The congregation is The Church of Our Saviour, The Rev. Newton Gordon Cosby, Pastor.

earthly predicament; God's word became real flesh and blood in Christ that the world in its totality may be reclaimed for him and become consciously again his world. God's incarnation is his own engagement with all secular forces. The Church of the Incarnation, out of divine necessity, is called upon to further the engagement for the sake of redemption.

Secularism is the Number One enemy of Western Christianity. It takes many forms. One is a philosophical attitude taken toward science by a band of philosophers known variously as Positivists, Physical Realists, Empiricists and a host of other names. Until recently they have generally controlled the departments of philosophy in the large universities. They are not scientists, though their general viewpoint is assumed by some scientists. In a much less technical sense the attitude filters down to the lay level and becomes part and parcel of the modern man's point of view. I refer to the position commonly called scientism which is not science but a caricature of it.

Scientism is a mood which is disposed to enthrone science as the God of our culture. In reality, it absolutizes the scientific method making it the sole criterion for arriving at Truth. "This is the truth, the whole truth and nothing but the truth." A thing is known only if it is known scientifically. Every other form of knowing is thereby abolished or "read off" as unauthentic. What cannot be verified by the scientific method is not necessarily false; it is simply meaningless. For the Christian to affirm that God is love is to talk not untruth but nonsense.

For science, the Christian must have profound respect. For the scientific attitude and the fruits of the scientific method, we are all indebted. But scientism, which owes any prestige it may profess to the results of science, as a philosophical attitude toward science, must be rejected as the god it makes itself to be. The kind of knowledge yielded by science, though attested and useful and even autonomous in its own sphere, is not the only knowledge nor is it saving knowledge for man. The problem of existence is not resolved by examining the theories and observations of physicists and astronomers. Philosophers of the "scientific outlook" are mostly non-scientists jumping on a scientific bandwagon as it makes its triumphal way down the modern avenue.

Scientism is a contemporary madness which has rapidly crept into popular thinking. If you can get things down into a formula, you can pretty much solve anything. It has had an eroding effect upon the significance of the Bible and the function of religion. It has created a popular mania for scientific proofs of the validity of the faith. In the adoration of the scientific method as the sole arbiter and guarantor of truth, the Bible is looked upon as antiquated and unscientific.

More tragically still, scientism as a cultural deity supplants Christian meaning. With the view that science alone can save us (scientism), the supernaturalistic view of the universe is replaced by a naturalistic philosophy of science. Moral and religious norms are swept aside and the ethical crisis of the West is deepened. A comment of the sceptic Bertrand Russell is worth citing: "It is a curious fact that just when the man on the street has begun to believe thoroughly in science, the man in the laboratory has begun to lose his faith." [31] A distinguished chemist wrote recently: "I think it is no exaggeration that in many areas, science is threatening to supplant religion as a guide of life; there is a great need for spiritual guidance (not the province of science) in an age when physical power stemming from science has grown as great as to threaten all life on earth." [32]

[31] Bertrand Russell, *The Scientific Outlook*, p. 88.
[32] Donald H. Andrews, *The Christian Scholar*, September, 1958, p. 360.

When the knowledge of faith is swallowed up in the knowledge of science (the great misunderstanding of the function of science), man is dehumanized and loses the meaning of his existence. Furthermore, God himself becomes an Object instead of the Subject he is, a truth to be searched for instead of the truth that searches. But God shines by his own light; the world (and science) by his reflected light.

3

CULTURED COMPETITORS

Put on your bifocals. We are going to move from West to East, from paganism near at hand to paganism far away, but not as far away as was once thought. Its centers of operation may be distant from American shores, but its significance touches every household of Christian faith at home. The problem posed for Christianity by the great non-Christian faiths is the problem of the Gospel's universality. It affects more than the specialist, since it reaches down to every parish pastor and family.

As exchange students from non-Christian lands come in numbers to American universities, the intercourse between faiths reaches beyond the abstract; it becomes as concrete (and valuable) as a classroom discussion and a dinner-table conversation. Christians, to whom the terms Buddhism, Hinduism and Islam were scarcely more than mythical a short time ago, are forced to examine their Christian faith in the framework of religious alternatives. Eastern faiths have flooded the paperback stands and popular pictorial magazines as well as the university courses in philosophy and religion with their doctrines. With the advent of the United Nations and diplomatic relations with the eastern countries have come also the interchange of cultural and religious ideas. The wall of isolation has been toppled and world religions, like other things, are in the open arena of discussion and debate, where, of course, they should be.

We have chosen to call these non-Christian faiths the "cultured competitors" of the Gospel. "Cultured," because not only do they represent many centuries of highly developed thought but also because their modern interpreters are often highly skilled, university-trained thinkers. Many have taken advanced studies in European universities and benefited from western cultural influences and Christian thought. I spent three hours with a young Buddhist scholar in the largest and most progressive monastery in Bangkok, who had just returned from four years of advanced study in a prominent Indian university and was well read in the writings of Brunner, Baillie and Tillich. A professor of Shinto received his undergraduate degree in divinity at the Chicago Divinity School. The scholarship of men like Radhakrishnan, Coomaraswamy and Suzuki is well-known and respected. True, there are vast areas of ignorance, superstition and religious primitivism where the Gospel has often made its most significant gains, as in the rural areas of India, but in the years immediately ahead, Christianity will be called upon to face its stiffest intellectual battles since the encounter of the early Church with the learned Greek pagan world. National programs of education and plans for religious instruction by the dominant religions will lift the level of appreciation and understanding of the traditional faiths.

These faiths are not just opponents. They are rivals or competitors. A significant change has taken place in the attitude of the non-Christian religious world with the transition from the nineteenth to the twentieth century. The change has been even more marked in the last two decades. The nineteenth century mood toward Christianity was colored by the political and economic fact of domination. The prevailing attitude was one of docility, passiveness, quiescence. With the coming of independence and nationhood, the mood changed to one of self-consciousness, self-assertiveness, aggressiveness, touched with not a little hostility. There is fast developing not merely a defense against

Christianity but a positive apologetic and a plan for missionary strategy rivaling that of the Christian mission. The non-Christian faiths are genuine competitors, a fact with which the younger Churches must deal realistically. The issue is more than academic; it may even be a matter of life and death.

Religious resurgence

The Asian world is in revolutionary transition. Any changes so catastrophic and far-reaching can be described as nothing less than a revolution. "The only possible parallels are the French and Russian revolutions and even they are dwarfed in comparison with the changes in Asia. Never before have so many millions of people taken part in such a rapid and radical social upheaval." [1] The revolution is simultaneously a reaction to western political domination, economic exploitation, western ideas of racial superiority and cultural domination and yet the appropriation of western cultural influences. Its major goals are political freedom, economic justice and social equality. The major problems are: the tension between traditional customs and western adaptations, the growth of national rivalries, the clash of rival ideologies, and the threat of communism. [2]

The resurgence of the traditional faiths cannot be understood apart from this revolutionary background. That the resurgence is real is indisputable. Shrines which had fallen into disuse are being rebuilt and refurnished and new shrines erected. The disestablishment of state Shinto has only hastened and expanded the activities of sectarian Shinto. Buddhist temples do a thriving business and gather consider-

[1] *Christianity and the Asian Revolution,* edited by Rajah B. Manikam, p. 3. A good study text on the social revolution in East Asia, the character of the resurgent religions and the state of the Church.
[2] *Ibid.,* pp. 4-12.

able funds. The largest temple in Tokyo has a staff of twenty-five full time priests kept busy in daily preaching and worship services, lecture courses, and counselling. An increasing number of courses are offered and elected in Shintoism and Buddhism in both religious schools and national universities. Communities of young scholars are diligently at work translating the sacred texts of the old faiths and providing more popular literature for the interested lay community. Everywhere one may see young and old visiting sacred places on pilgrimages and participating in large numbers at the seasonal festivals and celebrations. Doubtlessly spurred by Christian social concern, Buddhism has evidenced a very active interest in social and economic problems. Some have advocated more specialized training of Buddhist monks in the field of social welfare, though not without opposition from the more conservative ranks of Theravada Buddhist leaders. More progressive monasteries have sprouted as centers of education (both lower and higher) and social service. The monastery in Bangkok, for example, carries on an extensive educational program for the community, including a variety of courses in religious instruction.

In the background of this religious renascence stands a lively nationalism. For many of the young intellectuals, the interest is centered there exclusively. Nationalism becomes for them a religious passion and the traditional faiths hold little or no interest. They may acquiesce in religious festivals and maintain a passing deference for household religious rites, but essentially they are out-and-out secularists. Some even boldly affirm that the traditional faiths are a stumbling block to national progress and prestige in world affairs. But the more thoughtful and religiously sympathetic leaders, though sceptical about much of traditionalism, feel the need for a strong spiritually-cohesive center to the new nationalism, if for no other reason than to safeguard the nation against the outside threat of communism and the corroding influence of secularism within.

That the religious resurgence is to some degree a defensive action touched off by a suspicion and fear of Christianity need not be denied. Political nationalism alone cannot offset a dynamic religion like Christianity which admittedly has no political ambitions other than the desire to work for the best interests of enlightened nationhood. The real fear lies in a cultural imperialism considered every bit as dangerous as the only-too-recent political domination by the West. The advance of the Christian mission in such areas as evangelism, education, and social betterment, though often highly regarded and appreciated for the good that has been accomplished, (particularly in the latter two) is felt to be, nevertheless, by implication an undermining of traditional cultural patterns. The total confluence of ideas, including religion, from the West disturbs the East. The ancient culture has been shaken, body and soul. If the new nationalism is to be made solid, it must be buttressed by an equally renewed culture.

Just a word here about the oriental reaction to the Christian mission. The eastern world does not question the value of Christianity as a religion and its right to exist as an independent entity in a non-Christian environment. The Indian ambassador to the United States commented only recently that India takes pride in the fact that it is a land of many religious traditions and that Christianity has a time-honored position among them. A significant number of Indian leaders has profited from educational opportunities offered by Christian institutions. As recently as 1957, at least seventeen members of the Japanese Diet were Christians. I shared a room on the train with the mayor of the important city of Kyoto who was a Congregationalist.

The real concern of the eastern nations is over a Christianity that professes to be better than other religions and, more importantly, to be in possession of final and absolute truth. The latter point suggests the possibility of a goal of religious conquest and the eventual displacement of the old faiths and the cultures they created. In answer to the question, "Are there certain Christian ideas which tend to become major stumbling blocks to the acceptance of the Christian faith?", some of our missionaries replied that it is the "exclusiveness" of Christianity, "the idea that only through Christ can salvation come," which presents the biggest hurdle. Obviously this is more of an issue in lands with highly-developed cultures and among the educated who are more articulate in their religious thinking. Non-Christian religious leaders are quite sensitive at this point and make frequent reference to it in their writings and utterances. If Christian missions were to be very successful intellectually, it is feared that Christianity would be a serious threat both to established religion and culture. So the Christian movement becomes a goad to the religious resurgence in the East.

But we should badly misinterpret the renascence of the old religions were we to attribute it to a fear of Christian missionary enterprise. The explanation goes much deeper. Were it simply opposition from without, the nature of the renascence would result in defense and revival. It is that, but much more. It takes on the character of a reform and a reinterpretation. An internal dissatisfaction and upheaval is taking place within the ancient faiths themselves. Radhakrishnan writes: "If the living faith of the dead becomes the dead faith of the living our civilization will die. We must make rational changes . . . Life is not life unless it is thrusting continually into new forms." [3]

Hinduism, Buddhism, and to a lesser extent, perhaps,

[3] S. Radhakrishnan, *Religion and Society*, p. 107.

Islam (for it has already embarked on the journey), find themselves in much the same position that Christianity faced. Christianity fought out the battles with mathematical and empirical science, "higher and lower criticism," comparative philosophy, psychology and religion. By so doing, it saw the value of continuing intelligent self-criticism, pruned itself of indefensible accretions and prepared itself, as a living faith, to face the demands of a contemporary world. Not that the battle is ever ended. No form of Christianity can be said to have reached its fulfillment. It is an ever-continuing pilgrimage and the face-to-face encounter with other faiths and cultures is a major part of the struggle. Oriental religions stand at the threshold of intellectual self-consciousness and self-scrutiny, brought to that point by the awareness of their own spiritual inadequacies as much by the interplay of Western culture and the salutary influence of Christianity upon its life and thought. The forces are interrelated. Internal and external factors are not mutually exclusive. In this sense, the religion of the Gospel, even when not accepted, has rendered a service.

A new Hinduism is emerging in the minds of its intellectual leaders, vastly different from the old concepts and far removed from popular beliefs and practices. Though the thinking of leaders can normally be expected, in any faith, to travel ahead of the populace, in no religion is there such a wide discrepancy as in Hinduism. To move from the lecture hall in religion at the University of Calcutta to a rural village not too distant is like crossing a continent of ideas. This is in large measure due to the nature of Hinduism itself. It is peculiarly indefinable. When one has said that "Hinduism is the religion of the Hindus" that is about as exacting as one can get. He must proceed from that point into a description, historically and broadly, of all the widely diverse forms it takes from the primitively magical to the philosophically mystical. And all the forms are valid. The Indian mind is little disposed to pursue a rational formulation of religious truth. Hinduism is what each Indian believes, feels and practices. In that respect any intellectual confrontation of Christianity with Hinduism (and to a somewhat lesser degree Buddhism) must recognize immediately its limitations. Our Lutheran missionaries have vividly and correctly pointed that out. We are quite aware of it in these lectures. Any thorough treatment of the encounter demands an elaborate and quite specific analysis of the total Hindu religious mentality which takes one into all the areas of magic, animism, local religious customs, and cultic practices. And the nature of the confrontation must be determined by the form of Hinduism with which one is dealing.

I said that the wide discrepancy in ideas is due to the nature of Hinduism itself. But it is also the result of a low rate of literacy and the lack of educational facilities and means of communication. It may be assumed that, with independence and the elaborate plans for general education and rural reforms, the distance between university thought and the popular mentality will be greatly reduced. Hinduism will become less formless and primitive and more articulate. And each missionary must be increasingly better prepared to meet a more intellectually formidable faith.

It is natural for Neo-Hinduism to look upon the contemporary revolution in thought as nothing other than a modern restatement of traditional ideas. Because of the patternless character of the sacred writings, or rather, we should say, the multiform quality of their seemingly contradictory ideas (itself a pattern), the term "restatement" may have some justification. There is a remarkable elasticity in the Vedas, Upanishads, and Bhagavad-Gita. One can scarcely avoid the conclusion, however, that Mr. Radhakrishnan and others are not so much restating as "transposing" and rebuilding Hinduism into a modern universal and synthetic faith. Let us illustrate.

Modern reform movements have aimed sharply at the traditional caste system. The origins and description of caste are too vague and complex to be discussed here and are not germane to our purpose. Ideally, it was fashioned, over a period of centuries, to bring some order to the heterogeneous population of India by uniting that people in a common economic, social, cultural, and spiritual bond. Without debating it, it may be assumed that a number of values can be listed on the credit side of the caste system. [4] But long-range accounting is likely to find more on the debit side of the ledger. It turned out to be "the very antithesis of the principle of the essential equality of men . . . The caste system gave rise to serious social evils. It denied certain civil and religious rights to a large number of people and led to the oppression and exploitation of one class by another, which has proved a constant source of discontent and unrest . . . the gravest evil of the caste system is that it has rendered Indian society undemocratic and a sociological myth." [5] The lot of the exterior castes or outcastes was especially tragic, bringing all sorts of legal, social and religious disabilities. The constitution of the Indian Republic outlawed any discrimination on the grounds of religion, caste, sex or place of birth, abolished untouchability and forbade its practice. Injustices are far from rectified. The point is that the whole caste system and its subsequent abuses lay at the heart of the traditional Hindu religious system and was perpetuated by the fundamental doctrine of the eternal and inexorable law of karma. For many Hindus, rigid rules of caste were almost synonymous with Hinduism. The reform of the caste

[4] R. N. Dandekar, *The Religion of the Hindus,* edited by Kenneth W. Morgan, p. 143f.
[5] *Ibid.,* p. 149f.

system, therefore, can hardly be thought of as a "restatement" of traditional Hinduism. It may well mean the eventual and complete extermination of the system.

In the meaning of Reality and the Hindu view of life, the apologists of Neo-Hinduism have scored the most radical departures from traditionalism. Again these departures can scarcely be contained under the term restatement. In exchange for a traditionalism which held more or less in contempt the actual and historical world, treating it as essentially illusory, appears a new Hindu outlook or ideology which is very conscious of the physical and material world and India's destiny in world affairs. A world, which only recently possessed but a "dream-like" illusory reality [6] (maya), where the summons was chiefly to renunciation and withdrawal, has been transformed, in the new thought, into a world actively to be affirmed and exploited. "Leaders of Hindu thought and practice," writes Radhakrishnan, "are convinced that the times require not a surrender of the basic principles of Hinduism, but a restatement of them with special reference to the needs of the more complex and mobile social order." [7] But is this a restatement or a radical departure? Is Radhakrishnan reading "out of" or "into" basic and traditional Hindu principles? If it is the latter, as we think, then a new Hindu ideology is in the making and can hardly be defended on the basis of tradition. The real question then is, "will it be possible for Hinduism out of itself, unaided, to produce from its founts of religious theory an articulate, reasoned system, an adequate creed of belief—which will provide the needed intellectual justification and spiritual drive for a new

[6] "The appearance of the world is taken as real by the ignorant, but the wise who can see through it find nothing but Brahman, the only reality behind this illusory show. For the wise the world appearance is not real and Brahman is not the bearer of this illusion-producing power." S. C. Chatterjee, *Religion of the Hindus*, p. 239.

[7] S. Radhakrishnan, *Eastern Religions and Western Thought*, p. 130.

Hindu way of life." [8] I share the conclusion of Bouquet about Radhakrishnan that "in his role of apologist he does not represent Hinduism as it really is, so much as what he would like it to be and what he thinks he might be able to make it." [9]

This would seem the place to comment upon a fundamental, theological difference between Christianity and Hinduism, Buddhism and Islam. The concern of Christianity for the ills of the social order is not accidental. Though it has by no means succeeded in fulfilling its social responsibilities in the world, there is inherent in the Christian faith, rooted in the life and mind of Christ, a passionate concern about those conditions which produce inequities and atrocities and to which the conscience of the Church must constantly be directed. Not only the salvation of the individual but the transformation of that society in which individuals live and move and have their being is of primary concern. ". . . God so loved the *world*. . . . God was in Christ reconciling the *world*." The world is God's and because it is God's, by his grace it must be transformed and restored to him. Everything in it is precious to him and must be so to his children. Hospitals, schools, literacy, and institutions of social betterment are never secondary concerns of the overseas church. They are as primary as the proclamation of the Good News itself. Other faiths are not devoid of social concerns and can point, in principle and practice, to evidence of such sensitiveness, but the "world-transforming constructiveness" of the Christian movement and its dynamic for world-succor is nowhere to be matched in all the centuries. And for a fundamental reason, namely its essential world-affirmation. "This is our Father's world." By contrast, a comment of a noted Buddhist in a highly responsible government post is significant: "There

[8] *International Review of Missions*, Vol. 1939, p. 476.
[9] Alan C. Bouquet, *Christian Faith and the Non-Christian Religions*, p. 422.

is no organic link whatever between our fundamental Buddhist conception of life and the issues involved in modern society." [10] Everywhere I traveled through the entire non-Christian world, the one unanimous reply, made by non-Christian leaders to the question, "What do you think is the unique contribution, if any, of Christianity to your country?" was, "Its passionate concern for society."

Perhaps it should be noted that Hindu and Buddhist interest in ethics tends to be theoretical and individualistic, and, wherever unmodified by Christianity, socially passive and negative. Where it has led to the wider development of institutions for the handicapped and sick, it is the result indirectly at least of Christian influence. The social service work of the Ramakrishna Mission throughout India for the poor and afflicted, if not a denial, in practice, of the Hindu concepts of karma and samsara (reincarnation) is certainly a modification resulting from the Christian stimulus.

Buddhism, like Hinduism, in both its dominant forms—Theravada and Mahayana—is also challenged by the expansion of Christian missions as well as the urgency internally for facing up to the demands of the modern revolution in oriental life and thought. Beyond the fact of the theological reinterpretation of some of its fundamental concepts—karma and nibbana—two traits of revived Buddhism stand out, namely, the movements toward unity and world mission. These movements strikingly parallel and undoubtedly have been influenced by the twin movements in Christianity of unity and world mission.

The movement for Buddhist unity may seem somewhat surprising in the light of the vast differences in doctrine and outlook that exist in the two great branches of the faith. Indeed, Buddhism has often been considered not *a* faith but a family of faiths, capacious enough to gather within its fold

[10] *Ecumenical Review*, January, 1952, p. 124.

not only the many diverse strands of its own tradition but even ideas foreign to its thought, as, far example, primitive animism in Thailand, and Shinto and Confucian ideas in Japan and China. Though some Christian leaders are inclined to minimize Buddhist unity efforts as a purely "propaganda front" along with a "peace front" highlighted in the building of a Peace Pogoda at Hiroshima, the meetings of the World Fellowship of Buddhists in Ceylon (1950), Japan (1952), and Burma (1954) and the Sixth World Buddhist Council (1954) in Rangoon cannot be written off so lightly. The startling thing is that the initiative toward unity was taken by the conservative Theravada branch of Buddhism. Growing nationalism, the inroads of western culture and Christian missionary expansion call for a closing of ranks. Greater unity is seen to be a Buddhist necessity.

Equally significant is the Buddhist enthusiasm for world mission. An act of Parliament (1950) in Burma established the "Union Buddha Casana Council," one platform of which is the "propagation of the Dharma abroad." In Europe and the United States, Buddhist societies, made up not only of Far Eastern diplomatic and governmental representatives and orientals residing in the West, but increasingly of interested and religiously dissatisfied Westerners, are in the ascendancy. Many of the larger American cities, particularly New York, Chicago, and San Francisco, carry advertisements in their daily newspapers of Buddhist lectures and services. The Shin Sect (Mahayana) alone boasts of a hundred missionaries in the United States. World-wide Buddhist organizations and agencies like the Young East Association (Mahayana), the Maha Bodhi Society (Theravada), the Young Men's Buddhist Association, and the World Fellowship of Buddhists exist to propagate the faith. A growing interest in some kind of universal syncretistic faith for the solution of the world's ills, advanced most capably by scholars like Northrup, Hocking, and Toynbee, has opened up intellectual circles for the consideration of oriental philosophy and religion. Toynbee has set Mahayana Buddhism alongside Christianity as a live option among the redemptive religions. The highly eclectic and intellectually tolerant character of both Hinduism and Buddhism mark them as potentially strong missionary competitors of Christianity.

Principal competitors

We must now take a closer look at some of those rival faiths of the other-believing world, namely, Hinduism, Buddhism, and Islam, which present the greatest intellectual challenge to the Gospel. The Gospel is challenged by other religions and in other ways (e.g., religion in primitive societies, certain forms of Christianity itself) but the limitations of this series demand selection of material.

Our procedure will be to consider Hinduism and Buddhism together, not because doctrinally they stand together, though Buddhism has often been considered an heretical movement within Hinduism, but because they possess some primary philosophical traits and terms that place them together in a family of religious thought. In the consideration of these two traditions our plan is to approach them not by culling and then examining them doctrine for doctrine, but by evaluating their common dominant characteristics. We hope, thereby, to arrive more comprehensively at the essential "spirit" of these faiths and see it in relationship to the Gospel and Christianity. The problem of Christianity versus paganism is not a matter primarily of a conflict in "ideas" so much as a difference in mentality, point of view and outlook. Because Islam is "peculiarly" associated with Christianity and speaks a familiar language though it means something quite different, we shall consider it separately and briefly. Our thinking on Hinduism-Buddhism gathers about six characteristic traits.

1. Humanistic

We said previously that Hindu sacred writings are so diverse that they carry seemingly contradictory ideas and that there is a wide discrepancy of religious thought between illiterate India and the educated mind. Hinduism is conceived simultaneously as atheistic, non-theistic, theistic, pantheistic and supertheistic. Though not considered of equal merit, each is equally valid, depending upon the degree of competency and level of spiritual understanding. This is illustrated from a single paragraph in a modern Hindu author: "Philosophically, dualism between man and god is inadmissible, for essentially man is god. The very concepts of man and god cannot be said to possess absolute reality . . . That is why philosophical systems in India are essentially nontheistic or supertheistic . . . This does not mean that Hinduism has nothing to do with God. Hinduism, particularly popular Hinduism, is crowded with gods. Hinduism is certainly god-conscious, indeed very much so." [11] Again, "God is conceived as both personal and impersonal and as either identical with man and the world or both identical with and different from them. Whether such a view is or is not justifiable is an open question, but that it is not theistic in the accepted sense of the word will have to be admitted." [12]

In Hinduism, Reality is ultimately One and Spirit. Though it may be manifested in many forms or gradations —from matter to "beyond gods"—it is immanent, transeunt, transcendent. It is *something* (the word is significant) beyond

[11] Dandekar, *op. cit.*, p. 131.
[12] *Ibid.*, p. 238.

all its parts, yet evident in all parts. It pervades all. There can be no creation *ex nihilo* as an act; there can be only a dynamic activity of the One Spirit. Lower, popular forms of polytheistic Hinduism (Vishnuism and Civaism) may tend to individualize, objectivize and personalize this Spirit —and I think strike a greater truth than is realized, though the concepts arrived at are confused, shadowy, and mythological—but Reality is essentially impersonal and incomprehensible. Higher Hindu thought accepts popular Hinduism as a concession and inferior. Man is, in reality, one with God and salvation means overcoming ignorance and discovering the knowledge of that essential unity.

Now when Absolute Reality is conceived as impersonal it leads to a mystical or metaphysical humanism which negates God as self-existent. Hinduism is a magnified or cosmic humanism intuitively and mystically bent in upon itself and as such quite different from a western scientific and activistic humanism turned out upon its achievements. Man's center of interest is his "self." True knowledge is human self-knowledge. The way to such knowledge is by human searching. Man is the measure of all things. "Man himself is the architect of his life." [13]

Buddhism is also humanistic in its content and approach, but in a far different way, except in certain forms of philosophical Mahayanism where Buddhist thought approaches that of Hinduism. [14] Buddha himself had no apparent interest in the metaphysical or mystical but was much more concerned about the practical and urgent problems of human misery and suffering in the world. He had a special distaste for Brahmanism. The Buddhist sutras read like moral, psychological treatises of a humanistic nature with the goal of attaining a necessary "rightmindfulness" to drive out worldly

13 Dandekar, *op. cit.,* p. 128.
14 Coomaraswamy, *Hinduism and Buddhism.*

and carnal desires. In some respects Buddhism is a kind of religious counterpart of modern psychoanalysis and behavioristic psychology. It is a "psychological" humanism, a methodistic type of religious self-adjustment which every man must work out for himself. Since this world and everything in it, including man, exists as a continually changing process—there is no permanent "soul"—man must find a way of escaping or transcending it. In his noble Eightfold Path, Buddha devised a method, which, if faithfully followed, would bring deliverance from the rounds of rebirth. Nibbana is that "experience-event," that perfect rest and liberation from the tyranny of desire and its consequent suffering.

Man is his own saviour. The Buddhist Annual of Ceylon (1930) defined Buddhism as "that religion which without starting with a God, leads man to a stage where God's help is not necessary." A Buddhist friend once said to D. T. Niles, the great Ceylonese Christian, "You (Christians) are all damn cowards! You want God to do everything for you. He must save you; keep you; as for me I will save myself even if it takes a million births." [15] The primary mood of Buddhism is an aggressive vindication of man's self-sufficiency. Man can save himself from the sorrows of living by the process of self-renunciation. To be sure, in some forms of Mahayana Buddhism there is a tendency to deify Buddha as the Buddha nature or Buddhahood, but if the term "god" has any value it is primarily "poetical" to stand for the truth of man's real existence and fulfillment. Buddhism is the boldest of the oriental humanisms.

2. Subjectivistic

In his Gifford Lectures of 1947, Emil Brunner [16] discusses

---

[15] *International Review of Missions,* 1943, p. 258.
[16] Emil Brunner, *Christianity and Civilization,* pp. 30-44.

the relationship of Subject and Object in the understanding of Truth. He exposes the fallacies of both an extreme Objectivism and Subjectivism. Hinduism offers, perhaps, the clearest example of the latter. The most popular system of faith and philosophy in India today and gaining ground in the West is Advaita monism. It is the principle of the One Self, or Absolute Subjectivism. There is nothing which is "not self." The world which seems to stand over against the self, as an object, is only seemingly not-self. All is self. Therefore all pursuit of truth is the pursuit of self-knowledge. To engage in the knowledge of the universe, is to engage in the macrocosmic knowledge of one's self, for one's self is the universe in microcosm. The distinction between subject and object is unreal and illusory. The opposite of Hindu Idealism or Subjectivism are the twin-idolatries of Communistic materialism and scientism which tend to absolutize the objective world. The object is Truth or the knowledge of objective things is truth, Brunner declares. The shortcoming of Hindu subjectivism is that it takes little account of the world and offers little for the solution of world problems. The opposite fallacy of materialism is that it denies soul and impoverishes the spiritual life.

Buddhism is equally subjectivistic, not in a metaphysical, but in a psychological sense. It is introvertive, analytical, methodological, and obsessively concerned with the personal problems of desire and rebirth which bring suffering and sorrow. One suspects that Buddhism's teaching on compassion for others is more motivated by the removal of one's own desire than by genuine altruistic fellow-feeling. The tradegy of Buddhism is that it teaches love while it denies desire, yet love is the genuine desire that one's brother shall have what oneself has. The error lies in the Buddhist conception of desire. It is the selfishness of desire, "wrong" desires that must be overcome, not desire itself.

The Christian understanding of Truth lies neither in subjectivism nor objectivism. Neither mind nor the world is God. God is other than the mind or the world. The divine and the human are not merged but remain separate beings. Creation is not an "emanation" (Gnosticism) but an act or activity of God Who remains separate from it even when he initiates it. Knowledge of God is not achieved by self-knowledge. God is Subject and we are the objects of his redemptive love. To Hinduism, "Truth is God" [17] and the truth is self-knowledge; to Christianity, God is Truth, and not our conception of reality.

3. Individualistic

We only wish to observe here that the tendency in both Hinduism and Buddhism is to stress the loneliness of the journey toward enlightenment. Oriental mysticism with its yoga, meditation and ecstatic trance stresses the blessedness of being alone with "God" (the Self). The Buddhist would say: "The blessedness simply of being alone, of being withdrawn into oneself." [18] Theoretically, at least, the highest stage of life in Hinduism is still that of the religious hermit. A Burmese Christian in Rangoon commented: "Buddhism is a scheme of a lonely striving in an impersonal universe where people follow their separate and inexorable paths of destiny to fulfill the demands of an impersonal law." I saw the loneliness of this journey in a Bangkok monastery where guided by the abbot we saw the monks in their "cells" as they engaged in solo flights into meditation. An absolute idealism has a natural tendency toward some form of intense, radical individualism. A Buddhist friend said to Niles: "Salvation . . . must be sought by oneself through one's own

[17] S. Radhakrishnan, *Eastern Religions and Western Thought*, p. 313.
[18] D. T. Niles, *The Preacher's Task*, p. 65.

endeavor. (Buddhists) must think out for themselves the truth or falsity, reality or non-reality, the good and bad of all things . . . In Christianity, one prays to God as the Saviour and the dispenser of all good things in life. In Buddhism, each one is expected, by his own efforts, to ennoble himself in accordance with the Noble Eightfold Path. (Christianity) offers the doctrine of dependence in another as a child depends on the father. The doctrines of Buddhism, on the other hand, offer full independence and place full responsibility on each individual to earn his own desserts and work out his own salvation." [19]

Christianity speaks of the spiritual community of faith. Being a Christian is an intensely personal thing but never a private matter. One becomes a "Christian in community." Christ calls into community. Salvation is of God but from within the community of the redeemed. Nor does the Christian way lead toward solitariness. It enriches the life of society, gives new and deeper meanings to the circles of family and friendships and points to wider possibilities. The most difficult task of the Christian convert is to comprehend the meaning of the Church. The Church is the "communion of saints" not a gathering of individuals.

4. Non-revelatory

Hinduism speaks of the Vedas, the Upanishads, the Bhagavad-Gita, even the wooden and legalistic Brahmanas as divine revelation and looks upon them as the sacred scriptures from which all the diverse forms of Hinduism draw their inspiration. They are the "revealed writings." But "revealed" has a meaning quite different from that implied in the definition of the term. Revelation to the Hindu is not so much divine acts or activity toward man and the

19 Niles, *op. cit.*, p. 71f.

world as it is knowledge obtained from the insights of people who, by their own efforts, have intuitively grasped the truth of reality. Revelation is not divine self-disclosure but human self-discovery. The initiative is with man not God. When the line of differentiation between the human and the divine is erased and man fathoms the meaning of his own existence, he may be said to know or possess the truth. This knowledge he comes by not through a being outside or other than himself, nor through reason, but by an "experience" of spiritual illumination or intuitive apprehension. Sacred writings are guides in that they contain the experiences of teachers and saints who have attained. The ideal is to pass beyond the need of them.

Essentially, the same is true of Buddhism. The vast library of Buddhist sacred writings is, after all, the recorded experiences and insights of those who have followed the "Buddhist Path" and achieved enlightenment. Revelation is the result of human achievement. It is final self-liberation.

This conception of revelation is obviously quite different from the Christian and Jewish meaning or even the Moslem sense, though the latter differs widely from the Christian understanding. In the Christian revelation, God who is objectively other than man, the Absolute Subject, discloses himself to us. The revelation of God is not only a word from and about God but an action of God whereby he encounters us and makes his claim upon us. He calls, judges, forgives and saves us. Christian Truth is not merely propositional but living Divine Reality ("I am the Truth") confronting and abiding with men. To "know the truth" is not to accept certain propositions, however sublime, but to respond to the Truth, be in the Truth, love the Truth, walk with him who is the Truth. [20]

[20] Emil Brunner, *op. cit.,* p. 38f.

5. *Non-historical*

Though it must not be said that Hinduism and Buddhism have no interest in historical events nor a feeling of responsibility for what takes place in history, it can be said that neither of them has a sense of history or concern about the ultimate meaning of history. No great philosophies of history have come out of these religious traditions simply because the world has not been thought to possess any "real Reality." I say "real Reality" because, of course, the world has some reality, albeit shadowy. It has no genuine consciousness or ultimate significance. Salvation is essentially salvation "out of" or "from" the world. It is deliverance "from" eternal life (cyclic existence) not the Christian deliverance "to" eternal life. History is a nemesis to be transcended rather than the stage upon which the great drama of divine redemption is enacted. History is part of the meaningless, cyclical merry-go-round of birth, suffering, hardship, death, and rebirth. It is beginningless and endless, the goal of which is to fight one's way free of it.

The incarnations of Rama and Krishna may parallel historical figures (open to considerable question; Buddha Amitabha is certainly mythical), but their historicity is quite immaterial and inconsequential to the insights they represent. Both Hinduism and Buddhism stumble over a Christian emphasis upon the importance of a "truly historical incarnation."

The exploits of the pious king Rama and the princely Krishna may provide poetical and edifying fiction in a cyclic view of existence where their theophanies need periodic repetition, but these half-mythical avatars can have little redemptive value for those who take history seriously, who are caught in the struggles of history and who are concerned about the redemption of history. "No docetic deliverer can suffice for that. He can only show what mankind would like to happen, and what he shows is but a fantasy woven of wishful thinking." [21] Only One who is bone of man's bone and flesh of man's flesh can truly incarnate God and redeem history. A cheap incarnation may help to dispel ignorance; only a costly incarnation, with a price on its head, can overcome willful sin and death.

6. Syncretistic

The syncretistic character of Hinduism and Buddhism as of other oriental faiths is common knowledge. All naturalistic or cosmic "quests" for truth are essentially syncretistic. The so-called "new religions" of Japan and novel expressions of Hinduism, reflect this tendency to adopt, however contradictory, differing beliefs and practices. Hinduism with its capacious spirit is particularly conducive to such an eclecticism. Since no theological formulations on the nature of Reality can claim absolute validity (ultimate Reality is incomprehensible) then the sum total of partial understandings will add up to more than will the partial truth of any one faith. "Believe what you think you should about Ultimate Reality" (Devanandan). It is quite un-Hindu, even anti-Hindu to say, "What I believe is wholly true." Syncretism is the fruit of religious relativism. All religions or levels of religion are equally valid, though not equally worthwhile. Religious harmony, cooperation and unity will be found not in a common creed but in a common and sincere search. The World Congress of Religions and Radhakrishnan's proposal for a Parliament of Religions like a commonwealth of independent, equal nations spring out of this viewpoint. Buddhism like Hinduism is also a religious complex with the ability to baptize and integrate dissonant ideas and

[21] Alan C. Bouquet, *op. cit.*, p. 186.

traditions without shame of compromise or loss of integrity. The fact that some Eastern countries produce religious statistics exceeding the population figure is an expression not only of personal multiple-religious faith but a basic syncretistic tendency.

One readily sees the problems posed by a religion which makes a claim of finality as well as uniqueness for its message. "Theological exclusiveness" is the most critical charge that Oriental religion can level at Christianity. That charge must be given consideration in our next lecture.

Islam and Christianity

Islam and the Qur'an stand in a peculiar relationship to Christianity and the Bible. Notwithstanding the claims made by Moslems for the independent origin of the Qur'an, adducing that the suras were delivered inerrantly and directly from Allah to the Arabian prophet, most non-Moslem scholars believe that portions, at least, of the Bible existed in an imperfect and oral form and in that form influenced and are reflected in the suras. It is obvious from the frequent references to Christians as the "people of a book" that the Qur'an desired intensely their conversion, a conversion in great measure later accomplished.

Historians have often dwelt upon the phenomenon of the rapid and complete sweep of the Middle East into the Moslem orbit. The dynamic, fearless, even ruthless leadership of the prophet was a prime factor. The ground swell of Arab patriotism rising up for his support cannot be discountenanced. In his sensitiveness to and attack upon social inequities and degrading polytheism, Mohammad acted like a Hebrew prophet though surprisingly enough seemed to know little or nothing about them. It may not be pure speculation to assert that the triumph of Islam was the other side

of an early missionary failure of Christianity. A failure
doctrinally and ecclesiastically. The Church in the Byzantine
Empire weakened by heresies and torn by bickerings and
strife was in no condition to conquer Arabian paganism.
Islam was essentially a religious reform movement (Mohammad has been called an "Arabian Luther"), with some
parallel to Protestantism, but unlike Protestantism, became
a new faith because of an intense preoccupation with a single
dogma, namely that of the unity of God. This religious
paganism trampled idolatry but in so doing diminished the
nature of the godhead. The unity was secured at the expense
of the divine fullness.

The Moslem deity is a transcendent "other" God who has
no need to "disclose himself." He remains as inscrutable as
his ways. He sends messages, he establishes laws, he gives
directives from afar. His mode of revelation is an inerrant
book communicated verbatim to one messenger whose distinction lies solely in the fact that he was addressed. Nothing
must threaten God's unity and majesty, certainly not a
"personal" communication. Fellowship is not had on the
ground of his becoming man for the sake of man. It is not
the fellowship of father and son. It is the more stern relationship of master and servant based on sovereign will and the
command of unquestioning obedience. In a rigidly transcendent monotheism, the natural tendencies are toward
legalism, authoritarianism, externalism, predestinarianism.
The mysticism of the Sufi movement arose as an internal
reaction to bridge the Saviourless gap between a soverign
deity and his abject creatures, but its infiuence is slight and
not without its own peculiar aberrations and limitations.

4

CONTACT, CONFLICT AND ENCOUNTER

The meeting place today of Christianity and the non-Christian faiths is like that of the early Church in the learned and unlearned pagan world. As in the first five centuries Christianity, a minority religion, barely in its childhood, had to meet and overcome the national gods of the Greco-Roman world, polytheism in its many forms, the entire assortment of mystery cults and the more advanced philosophies like Stoicism and Neo-Platonism; today, still a minority faith, Christianity confronts the great religions and philosophies of the East. In some respects, of course, the situation is altered. The centuries have given Christianity age, success, and prestige. Christianity has mothered an advanced culture and created an environment out of which has come a world-embracing scientific and technological revolution. But its minority status has not changed and stands to deepen with the rapid population increase in the Orient. Though not persecuted, it frequently meets up with hindrances, hostility and occasionally reprisals. The extreme religious diversity and intensified nationalism of the Eastern world recalls a similar complexity in the Roman Empire of earlier times.

It must be kept in mind that the ecumenical problem is more than one of religious encounter. The larger focus is the whole Oriental world and man in that world. The Gospel was sent to "the world." Therefore, the whole cultural world —political, economic, social, aesthetic, moral—is the object of the Church's message. The "world" is to be redeemed. With characteristic insight, D. T. Niles says: "The Christian message is not addressed to other religions, it is not about other religions; the Christian message is about the world. It tells the world a truth about itself—God loved it and loves it still. It is well to remember that the world is non-Christian only in a historical sense. It is already in God's purpose a world for which Jesus died and over which he rules." [1] Our attention is centered upon the religious milieu of the East, not because it can be neatly isolated and examined as part of Oriental culture, but because it rests at the center of that culture, more integral to it than Christianity in the West.

Two critical appraisals

To help get the problem of Christianity's confrontation with non-Christian faiths into focus, let us summarize briefly the thought of two distinguished contemporary theorists, the one an American professor of philosophy and law, the other an Indian social historian. The fact that neither is a professional theologian or "scientist of religious thought" may appear to lessen their value for us, though they are both men of broad and profound learning; but, on the other hand, because they are not theologians their thinking may strike more comprehensively at the issues involved.

Professor Northrop of Yale University in his book *The Meeting of East and West* [2] attempts philosophically to bridge the great gulf between the eastern and western world. He contends that the bridgework must be done for the sake of world understanding and peace and that it must be a matter of aesthetic appreciation and acceptance of the diverse cul-

---

[1] Niles, *op. cit.*, p. 89f.
[2] His later work, *The Taming of the Nations,* also touches upon the subject but deals more specifically with the cultural basis of international policy.

tures and the recognition of the validity of the moral, philosophical, religious, artistic and scientific contributions of each. The East and West must meet at the highest levels possible and enter into a thorough discussion of their distinctive cultural continuums.

In the attitude of both traditional and liberal Christianity he sees a great bone of contention. Christian theism believes that God has fully and finally revealed himself in Jesus Christ. Since there can be no greater revelation of God than his own self-disclosure, this Christian conviction creates immediately a point of tension between the Christian and the vast non-Christian world. Other views of Reality are of less value if not altogether valueless and untenable. Friction, disdain, animosity, superiority and suspicion follow. "One tends to be untrue to one's religion if one admits any truths or values in any other religion which one's own theistic religion does not possess. When to this is added the injunction from the Saviour to spread his perfect gospel throughout the world, the cooperative spirit is not helped particularly. Instead, an aggressive missionary evangelism is added to a self-righteous religious perfectionism and provincialism." [3]

If the conflicts and prejudices of the world are to be ameliorated in the West as well as the East, a much more penetrating reformation than that of the sixteenth century "with respect to the sufficiency and the authority of the claims of the theistic religions must occur. One of the major causes of the ills of our world has its source in very high places." [4] Northrop then proceeds to point out that it is not only the exclusiveness and finally of certain theistic religions (Christianity, Islam) which creates the unnecessary tension but also their insistence upon the specificness, determinateness and absoluteness of Reality (God) with correspond-

[3] F. S. C. Northrop, *The Meeting of East and West,* p. 413.
[4] *Ibid.,* p. 413f.

ing rules and laws. Contrasted with this point of view is a Hindu orthodoxy and a general Far-Eastern aesthetic indeterminate, non-theistic religious type which is open-minded and hospitable to other religious groups and ideas. Clearly the burden of guilt rests upon the western monotheisms, particularly Christianity. Shridharani voices a similar protest: "The very notion [of missionary evangelism] implies a superiority complex as well as an impulse of self-righteousness. It looks very strange to the Hindu. One cannot describe it [evangelism] as a desire to share things that are personally precious. Such a desire would turn into fellowship, into discourse, never into a drive for conversion. I feel that all the great religions have one thing to learn from Hinduism: a humility born of a profound philosophic insight into the relativity of knowledge of ideals. Exclusiveness is antispiritual inasmuch as it is overweening in the light of the limitations of human perception." [5]

Northrop appeals, therefore, for a catholicity of spirit that recognizes the equal validity of two religious types. Appreciation and acknowledgement of each's contribution to truth will lay the ground for world understanding and peace.

Now whatever else may be made of Northrop's claim certain things are quite obvious. The Church believing what it does has not always bothered greatly to understand or care what the non-Christian world believed. There seemed little reason to. Consequently, there developed between the communities a wide span of ignorance and misunderstanding. And ignorance is a breeder of suspicion and tension. Basically, Northrop is correct if one is careful to differentiate between personal attitudes and the fundamental Christian message. The Gospel has always been an offense, including an offense to religion. And, paradoxically, the "exclusiveness"

[5] Krishnalal Shridharani, *My India, My America*, p. 338.

of Christianity's message is the source of its peculiar universality. To this we must return.

The second of the critical appraisals comes from K. M. Panikkar in his *Asia and Western Dominance,* particularly his chapter on "The Failure of Christian Missions." Most Christians are not likely to accept his stinging statements, though they must be examined in any event, because they reflect a definite Asian viewpoint. They are the reflections of a much-traveled, perceptive analyst. In Panikkar's judgment, Christian missions in India today are rather insignificant except in the fields of education and medical services. The reason for the failure of missions (he assumes a large degree of failure) in the Far East, he attributes to the following causes:

1. Western missionaries brought to the East an attitude, consciously or unconsciously, of moral superiority and a belief in their own exclusive brand of righteousness. To the Hindu who believes that all good ways lead to God (Reality), and to the Buddhist who is taught that the practice of the Eightfold Path will perfect him, the claim of any votary or sect that it alone has the truth seems unreasonable and absurd.

2. Until the end of World War II, the association of Christian missions with aggressive western imperialism introduced political complications into Christian work. [6] National sentiment looked upon missionary endeavor as inimical to the country's interest and native Christians as "second rate" citizens or "secondary barbarians."

3. Missionaries, consciously or unconsciously, brought with them not only the Gospel which is final but the sense of an European superiority which produced an inevitable reaction.

[6] A little more than a year ago, the Indian ambassador speaking to a group of Washington churchmen made a similar reference to the association of missions with colonialism and the obstacles created by a rising Oriental nationalism.

Even in missionary schools where literature was taught, it was always European literature, European or Western history, philosophy and art. Christians by their curricula virtually identified themselves, in Panikkar's eyes, with Western imperialism. Educational activities, far from helping the cause of the Christian faith, only led to the identification of the work of Christian missions with "western and American cultural aggression."

4. A basic cause for missionary failure was the wide variety of Christian sects which came to practice in the East—from Roman Catholicism to Seventh Day Adventism—each proclaiming the errors and superstitions of the other to the embarrassment of the whole missionary movement. Christian missions may one day be renewed and successful but the favorable atmosphere of the 19th century will not return in the 20th or in any future century.

However critical and unjust these two appraisals may be —and the second is more characteristic of an extremist and earlier attitude—they do, in fact, reflect much of contemporary thinking in the East. This must be acknowledged and counteracted by an intelligent witness to the Gospel. The encounter of Christianity with non-Christian faiths must be looked at closely and understandingly.

Christian approaches

The Christian engagement of the non-Christian faiths raises fundamental questions. What is truth in religion and how can it be known? Can it be known in somewhat the same manner that world truth is known, and if so, what of the meaning of revelation? Is revelation to be understood as the independent activity or communication of the Divine toward the human whereby the Divine becomes not an object of man's quest but the subject of redemptive activity; or must

revelation be considered in a more comprehensive sense find-
ing expression in human thought and activity not only
toward God but toward one's self and the world? How are
we to deal with similarities of ideas as well as radical differences between religious systems? Are there bonafide bases
for theological cooperation and encounter in the problem of
religious truth or does a principle of discontinuity obviate
this possibility? Granted a uniqueness about the Christian
message in what does this uniqueness consist? Does it also
imply finality and exclusiveness and thus preclude any
serious consideration of other beliefs? What attitudes *may*
(or does the Gospel dictate *must*) Christian thought take
toward non-Christian faiths?

With some notable exceptions, Christians have not crossed
over the intellectual frontiers into the realm of other religions. While the early Church produced its Origens, Cle-
ments and Augustines who in the classic words of T. G.
Glover "outthought their contemporaries" in the citadels of
learning, the modern Church has yet to meet paganism effectively on the high ground. One seasoned missionary commented that he knew of no first-class theologian in Oriental
Christianity. There may be at least a hidden truth in the jibe
of the non-Christian critics: "Having been foiled in their
assault on the real strongholds of Asiatic life, Christianity
dodges obstacles by making an approach, often successful, to
simple people lacking a clearly-defined faith which can withstand Christianity." [7] Not that the world is saved by thought.
The secrets of the Kingdom are often hidden from the wise
and prudent and revealed unto babes (Luke 10:21). And
Christ is the Saviour of the unlearned and primitive too. But
if the Gospel is the redemption of all religion, then one
prerequisite, at least, of such redemption must be a thorough-

[7] *Ecumenical Review,* Autumn, 1948, p. 73.

going knowledge of those faiths in the context of the Gospel. How shall we look upon the rivals of the Gospel?

1. Rejection

On both a priori and a posteriori grounds some Christian thinkers rule out truths in other religions and so categorically reject all other faiths. [8] If Christ is the only way, truth, and life, he alone is saviour of the world; if Christianity is the only bonafide universal faith, then by definition and basic assumptions, any and all other faiths must be discarded. By this approach, other religions are often rejected without even seriously examining them. The belief is that there is no need to examine them. And where they are examined it is primarily for the purpose of refutation and conquest. It must be said that devout Christians have espoused this position in a passionate concern for the rescue of all the heathen. At times distinguished "heathen" themselves having once embraced Christianity adopted this approach. The Indian Sanskrit scholars, Nehemiah Goreh and Pandita Ramabai, after conversion, acknowledged their former religion as all unqualified error and untruth. [9]

This way is essentially dogmatic and has been largely discredited or invalidated as a method. For one thing, a fuller knowledge and appreciation of non-Christian faiths has convinced the thinking Christian that they deserve something better than to be cast summarily upon a theological ash heap. One does not have to become a Hindu or Confucianist to realize that there is much of spiritual and ethical value there, however it may have got there. Acceptance of

[8] For a full treatment of the approaches to non-Christian faiths see E. C Dewick, *The Christian Attitude to Other Religions;* for a good summary analysis of individual viewpoints read J. R. Chandran's article in *Christianity and the Asian Revolution,* pp. 185-209 and A. C. Bouquet, *The Christian Faith and Non-Christian Religions,* pp. 335-423.
[9] J. R. Chandran, *op. cit.,* p. 188.

the Gospel is not the baptism of Hinduism, but then nothing
that is precious is ever lost. It must be laid at the feet of
Jesus. Every convert, in point of fact, brings something of
his heritage into Christianity with him. The Gospel separates the dross. And the process of separation is an endless
one. Bold rejection, particularly without examination, leads
only to hostility and reaction not to receptivity and acceptance. It is, as Dewick states, an "answer of war." [10]

2. Co-existence

The International Missionary Council at Jerusalem
(1928), though it placarded the slogan "Our Message is
Jesus Christ," opened the door for a more thorough and
sympathetic approach to the study of non-Christian faiths.
If the Gospel is to be brought to the other-believing world,
ways must be found effectively to do it. Considerable scholarship had already been undertaken, independently of the
Church, in Western universities by "objective" scientists of
religion. A very sympathetic (but highly controversial) point
of view was advanced in the so-called Report of the American Laymen's Commission, *Rethinking Missions* (1932), the
principal architect of which was the distinguished Harvard
professor of philosophy, William E. Hocking. A fuller statement of that position appeared later in his two books. [11]

The thinking of the Commission was rooted in a "liberal
theology" which generally discountenanced the emphasis on
church dogma and gave high value to the example and
teaching of Jesus. Briefly summarized the report noted: Any
western Christianity is foredoomed and must go. It is im-
perative that Christianity be presented in terms which those
wholly unfamiliar with the history of Christian thought can

[10] E. C. Dewick, *op. cit.*, p. 40.
[11] *Living Religions and a World Faith; The Coming World Civilization.*

understand. Non-Christian faiths need not be wholly discarded nor is a religious synthesis feasible. Rather, each religion must discover, by way of "reconception," its essential qualities through a careful, sympathetic knowledge of other faiths. One can be enriched by the other. The criteria for evaluating religious truth are reason and the study of comparative religious experience. Hocking sees the necessity for the emergence of a world faith and ways to achieve it. Progress may be made only if the great religions renounce the attitudes of intolerant exclusiveness and radical replacement. Christianity, which in many ways is superior to other religions, has a prominent role to play in the emergence of this world faith. But Christianity does not stand in a class apart, providing the only way to the salvation of mankind. In principle, all religions meet at dead level. Each must be respected and be true to its best self while not refusing to grow by "reconception."

There are a number of fallacies and blind spots in the Hocking approach. That each religious faith may see itself more clearly through religious intercourse may be granted. It is even highly desirable. But an important question is, what constitutes Christianity? Hocking has his own ideas, and apparently they do not include the biblical conception that God himself acted in a unique and final way in Christ. Professor Farmer raises the point: "Can Christianity remain true to itself while giving up the claim that Christ is in some quite final manner the only way?" [12] What disposition is to be made of the statement of Jesus: "I am the way, the truth, and the life; no one comes to the Father, but by me" (John 14:6)?; and the faith of the disciples: "And there is salvation in no one else, for there is no other name under heaven given among men by which we must be saved." (Acts 4:12) They must either be explained or explained away if Christianity

[12] *International Review of Missions,* 1941, p. 262.

is to be true to itself. That Christ held the conviction that the kingdom of God broke into history in a unique and final way in himself cannot be easily set aside. The attention he deliberately drew to himself is embarrassing if regarded as unexceptable or peripheral in importance. It is precisely the "essential" qualities in Christianity that bring it into conflict with other faiths and tend to disqualify it from active participation in the formulation of a new world faith.

Hocking is convinced that the trend is decidedly in the direction of a "single world religion," that such a religion will come about through global consultation, reconception, and agreement, and that Christ will be the prominent figure in the faith that finally emerges. While the Laymen's Commission Report was generally unacceptable to the major denominational bodies, it influenced and sparked a number of independent writings on the subject and undoubtedly helped to broaden missionary philosophy and practice. At any rate, it set the stage for the most controversial of all books in the field and brought forth the most provocative of missionary theologians.

But first a brief reference to Arnold Toynbee. In both his Gifford and Hewett [13] lectures, particularly the latter, Toynbee gives attention to the conflict of religions. He concludes that the two faiths best prepared to meet the deepest needs of mankind are Mahayana Buddhism and Christianity. But he feels Christianity must undergo two changes. It must be purged of its Western accessories which only weaken its witness in the eastern world and it must be purged of a traditional belief in its own uniqueness. After the manner of Radhakrishnan, he expresses great concern for the need of tolerance, a tolerance alone that recognizes that men are united in a common quest to understand a mystery. We are

[13] Arnold Toynbee, *An Historian's Approach to Religion,* and *Christianity Among the Religions of the World.*

more united in our questing than divided on our differences. We are all spiritual brethren. Tolerance is perfected through love. Toynbee appears to confuse "tolerance of truth" with tolerance as a spiritual virtue. In the latter case one must go further than Toynbee and speak not of tolerance in religion but freedom of religion.

3. Dialogue

The Jerusalem Council (1928) led to "Rethinking Missions," which touched off Hendrik Kraemer's *The Christian Message in the Non-Christian World* and the debates at the International Missionary Council of Tambaram, Madras (1938). Kraemer, without doubt is the foremost missiological apologist of our time. More than any other he has sharpened the focus and presented the intellectual issues involved in the encounter of world religions. [14] We have space only to present his principal lines of argument.

In his criticism of Radhakrishnan, Kraemer indicates in a sentence the motivation which has made him such a biting apologist: "What is needed in the present time of world encounter of religions is not to be as sweet as possible with each other but to learn the art of being as true as possible with each other in spiritual emulation." [15] Two major theses guide his earlier work: (1) Biblical Christianity presents God's revelations in Jesus Christ as God's solitary act for the redemption of mankind and therefore as a life or death crisis of all religions (Kraemer's idea of "biblical realism"); (2) the scientific study of world religions forbids us from conceiving any relationship of preparation and fulfillment between these religions and the revelation in Jesus Christ

[14] Beyond his study book for Madras, Kraemer has further enlarged and clarified his thought in *Religion and the Christian Faith* and numerous articles in the *International Review of Missions*.
[15] Hendrik Kraemer *Religion and the Christian Faith*, p. 134.

(his principle of "discontinuity"). The centrality and primacy must be given to God's revelation of himself and his initiative in seeking men. The starting point is not intuition, divination, religious consciousness or reason but God's self-disclosure in Jesus Christ. The a priori for the Christian is allegiance to Christ. The starting point for man, therefore, is faith, i.e., response to what God has done. In that response of faith, the act of will must take precedence over the intellect [Kraemer criticizes Aquinas for an overemphasis on the intellect].

In any such encounter, truth must be a prime prerequisite. We must rise above fairness and unfairness. Everything must be seen and judged in the face of Jesus Christ, the most merciful and severe judge. The right theological criterion for evaluating truth is not some "universal idea" of religion but God's revelatory act in Jesus Christ. [16] Kraemer is particularly critical of the Jerusalem Council (1928) for assuming that there was such a "universal idea" of religion, not for the fact that it recognized values in other religions. Christ is the judge over all religions including empirical, contemporary forms of Christianity. Though Kraemer in his later work softens an earlier statement that other religions are purely "human achievements," he nevertheless maintains that "there is a great amount of human achievement in all religions," [17] and at any rate there is no continuity of preparation and fulfillment between the Gospel and religions. Not that God is in no way active in these religions but we cannot clearly understand what he is saying or doing.

Bultmann echoes the thought of Kraemer, but in a slightly different way when he observes that Christianity, in a parallel sense, as a religion among religions, establishes an inevitable

[16] This is H. H. Farmer's principal presupposition in his theological study of religion, *Revelation and Religion.*
[17] Kraemer, *op. cit.,* p. 8.

contact with all other faiths. As a system of doctrine, tradition, cultic practice, and organization, it is part of the continuous story of religion. But when one thinks of the Gospel itself and other religions there is only conflict and encounter. If Christian theology thinks of Christian faith not as a phenomenon of the history of the human mind, or of religion at all, but as the answer to the question put to man through a particular revelation of God, there is then manifestly no continuity between Christian and non-Christian religions. God's activity in Christ conflicts with all men and in their religion at that, but in that very conflict the real point of contact is created. It is created by God. It is man in his existence, not in his intellectual life and history only that God addresses in the Gospel. [18]

Kraemer's works have provoked a flood of articles and books in debate. In his massive analysis he has not only served to clarify the intellectual issues involved in the relation between Christianity and non-Christian faiths, but has stimulated the kind of theological dialogue which must be carried on in any truly ecumenical Christianity. Ignorance among Christians (even leaders) of the content and claims of other religions as well as outdated and unsympathetic interpretations of their beliefs and practices can only be dispelled by intensive and systematic study. The resulting knowledge can throw real light on the great essentials of Christian faith itself. There is a truth in Max Muller's comment that "he who knows only one religion knows none." We are all debtors to Kraemer. Full dialogue, of course, must be carried on by our missionaries at the frontiers of the pagan world and more specifically by gifted Indian, Japanese, African, and all Eastern Christian leaders themselves. Such dialogue will take into account all the varieties

[18] R. Bultmann, *Essays Philosophical and Theological*, p. 133f, Macmillan, 1955.

of non-Christian religious expression and deal with each separately. It will clarify religious terms used, especially those used interchangeably by Christian and non-Christian and in the long process will discover the place and possibility of a genuine indigenous Christian expression of the faith committed to the Fathers.

Fundamental issues

Kraemer has forcefully defended the central claim of evangelical Christianity, namely, the absolute character of Christ and the Gospel as the criterion for the understanding of religious truth. And Christians must be bold enough to call all men out of their faiths and unbelief to faith in Christ. Christ is the unique and final revelation of God. Kraemer is quite correct also, I believe, in sharply differentiating between all religions of questing and feeling which proceed from man, and that religion whose message is rooted in the mind, heart, and activity of God. God will not be known nor will man be saved after the fashion of a Laymen's Inquiry whereby all faiths unite and press forward to the discovery of the New Testament of every existing faith. The Gospel is not comparative religion, indeed not religion at all. Kagawa once commented that "Christ would not have been crucified if he had preached comparative religion." Any study of religions which calls for a modification of Christ has little value for the Christian. Men may "trip over the truth" in Christ, he may become the stone of stumbling, but the shape of the stone cannot be changed. [19]

Granted Kraemer's main thesis, a big question still remains whether he has not been unnecessarily extreme and arbitrary in his understanding of "biblical realism," revelation and "discontinuity." Has he not in practical effect tended

[19] Niles, *op. cit.*, p. 14.

to close doors, not open them, in communication and dialogue, notwithstanding his vast knowledge of world faiths?
Not that he is wholly unaware of lofty developments in
pagan thought: "God forbid that we should be so irreverent
as to dispose of how and where the sovereign God of grace
and love has to act." But if God is continuously occupying
himself and wrestling with all peoples, with man in all ages,
then no religion, even the most primitive, can be merely a
product of the human mind. There must be in them something which comes from beyond nature and man. The God
of redemption and sanctification cannot be so sharply separated from the God of creation. Such passages as Romans
1:19, 20; 2:14, 15; Acts 14:17 and 17:27 cannot be explained,
apart from the view of God's mysterious though "hidden"
working in human experience. If God has not left any people
alone, without a witness of himself, must not that fact be
understood as his own activity? Would mankind have forever
groped, however blindly, after him unless they were endowed
with some sense that he was there to be found? Can there be
any knowledge of God which has not come from his spirit;
for not only is man unable by searching to find out God,
but without God he would not even follow the ceaseless
quest? The quest may not lead to God—and truth is something other than questing—but truth cannot be imparted to
non-questing and the questing is of God. "No man's religion
and no religious system is purely a product of man. To say
that they are, is to deny that man is made in God's image." [20]
To deny this as genuine divine communication in human
experience and a kind of *preparatio evangelica* is virtually
to close doors to the Gospel conquest of the world.

All Christians must assume that the self-disclosure of God
in Christ is the standard by which all truth is finally to be
tested, and no other category of religious truth except that

[20] Niles, *op. cit.,* p. 92f.

in the biblical disclosure can be normative. But it must be borne in mind that there are divergent views about the nature and content of that Christian revelation itself. Every presentation of the "normative Gospel" is colored by the sinful, errant, imperfect human element, unless, of course, we are prepared to accept the doctrine of an infallible agent (Church). The Gospel in itself is absolute for it is God's own "Good News;" but the empirical church as proclaimer and interpreter introduces the element of the relative. Therefore, the Christian dialogue with other faiths may, in the providence of God, play an important part in the cleansing of empirical Christianity.

One must undoubtedly differentiate between that fullness of revelation in the incarnate, redeeming Christ and the "hiddenness" of God's witness of himself outside the historical Jesus, but to speak of the two as "absolutely discontinuous" is virtually to divide God and separate Creator and Redeemer. Standing in the middle of the Areopagus, Paul perceived that the Athenians worshipped an unknown God (Acts 17:23). Revelation (in Christ) made intelligible the object of the pagan worship. Christ was the redemption of their ignorance and the purification of their worship. But the spirit of God already was at work in their act of worship, however ignorantly executed because of sin and darkness; and Christ produced a radical turn and fulfilled the deepest Athenian desire; he did not simply complete their incomplete ideas. There is continuity in the Spirit there, not "absolute discontinuity." Perhaps in the call to worship, not in creed and systems, Christianity may find the deepest measure of affinity with the non-Christian world. There may well be a life "hid in God" (A. G. Hogg) which has not yet grasped hold of truth in Christ and so wanders about in uncertainty. Can this life be "totally discontinuous" with God's full self-disclosure?

We spoke previously of the similarity of situation of the modern church and the Early Christian community. This is especially true as regards pagan syncretistic tendencies. As the primitive church lived in a Hellenistic-Oriental environment clothed in syncretism, so contemporary Christianity must work in the highly syncretistic atmosphere of Asia. One missionary tersely commented that "syncretism in India is too well known to enlarge on it." Another wrote that it is "becoming more and more popular and very difficult to combat." Still another referred to popular pictures quite common in India (I, too, saw them) of Gandhi surrounded by the Buddha, Krishna, and the crucifixion. In Hindu homes, pictures of Christ hang next to pictures of Hindu deities. This is not new. What seems to be new is that syncretism tends to become "official" and is propagated and promoted in high quarters. [21] Along with it goes considerable theological promiscuity.

Syncretism finds a most pointed expression in a movement grounded on the conviction of the essential oneness of the different religions of the world. This unity must "be broadened to include what a reader finds good in the best conception of Brahma in India, of the Supreme Spirit of Enlightenment of Buddhism, of Allah in Mohammedanism, and the oneness of God in the highest Greek philosophy and in modern science." [22] It is the central theme of the International Congress for the History of Religions. A report of the University Education Commission appointed by the government of India (signed by six Indians, one British, two American professors, and the chairman, Radhakrishnan) proposed that "what is good and great in every religion and what is more essential, the unity of all religions" should be presented.

[21] *Ecumenical Review*, Spring, 1950, p. 233.
[22] Lawrence Faucett, *Six Great Teachers of Morality*, p. 4. Quoted from *Japanese Religions*, a quarterly.

St. Paul's text: "Do you not know that you are God's temple and that God's Spirit dwells in you," is only a variant of the famous Hindu text, "Tat Tvam asi," meaning "that art thou." [23] Niles quotes a Hindu as saying: "We shall put an image of Christ into every Hindu temple and then no Hindu will see the point of becoming a Christian." [24]

Against this Oriental tendency toward a "syncretistic unity" the "exclusivism" of Christianity's message appears most unfavorable. To the Oriental, Christianity is the worst offender. Christianity is "essentially exclusive" for it sees no unity between the Gospel and religions. The Gospel is a scandal to common denominator religion. It can brook no traffic with religious relativism. Christians must accept the charge and continue to preach the "foolish" Gospel. A young missionary states: "Since we believe that salvation lies in the exclusiveness of Christ we might as well devote ourselves to affirming it with all that is in us. If others are truly brought into confrontation with him then Christ will speak for himself."

But we must make several important observations about that "exclusivism." For one thing the exclusiveness is in Christ, not in us. It is not an exclusive "attitude" but an exclusive "message." Empirical Christianity is not the absolute "way, truth, and life"—Christ is. He is the judge of all religions, not we. The real conflict between religious syncretism and Christian exclusivism can only become creative as Christians enter fully into the spiritual struggles of the non-Christian world, not only bearing witness to the Gospel, but coming to grips with the religions themselves.

The other side of exclusiveness is paradoxically the true universality of the Gospel. The one unerring way to the Father is the Father's perfect way to us. Listen to our missionary: "I believe that it is *because* of the uniqueness of Christ

[23] *Ecumenical Review, op. cit.*, Spring, 1950, p. 233.
[24] Niles, *op. cit.*, p. 17.

as the incarnation of God that Christianity can be a world religion. And it is only *because* the son of God is exclusive, that it is possible for anyone in the world to stand before God in the relationship of I-Thou and know him. And love him. And herein lies the highest peace and happiness of any human creature."

Syncretism is a mortal foe of the Gospel and must be firmly resisted. The International Missionary Council at Willingen (1952) stressed the rampant danger of its religious relativism and the need to affirm unequivocally the Lordship of Christ. But there is a clear difference between syncretism and adaptation as Kraemer clearly points out. [25] Adaptation may lead, sometimes almost unconsciously, into syncretism, but adaptation is essential if the Gospel is to be communicated to a world "dominated by non-Christian philosophies and cultures." There are right and wrong ways of interpreting the Christian faith. Syncretism is wrong where "the philosophy with which the Gospel is yoked is in essential conflict with the Christian revelation." [26] Christians must possess the boldness and wisdom of an Apostle Paul who ventured into pagan territory and preached the Gospel in Greek terms but in terms redeemed with the content of the "foolish" Gospel; into the syncretistic, cosmological categories of the Colossians, rethinking them in the light of Christ and the Christocentric way. In that way the Gospel was made endemic, relevant, and universally-particular. It was no longer foreign. Any bold venture is risky according to Kraemer but the danger must not be avoided at the expense of the failure to meet, in living encounter, the deepest needs of mankind.

Asians and some Westerners do not tire of pointing out the contrast between Oriental tolerance in religion and Christian intolerance. The observation is unhappily true

[25] Kraemer, *op. cit.*, Chapters 24, 25.
[26] J. R. Chandran, *Student World*, p. 341, 1958.

in one sense and grossly untrue in another sense. It is true in the sense that Christians themselves are, at times, intolerant in the same manner in which divisions result in divisive spirit. The "intolerance of the Gospel" is not synonymous with an "intolerant spirit." An intolerant spirit can only be broken down on the confession that though "Christ is Truth" the truth is not in us. As H. G. Wells once said, "The truth in the Galilean has been too great for our small hearts." An "intolerant Gospel" must be proclaimed by humble, contrite, and loving hearts.

But in the context of our thought, the Asiatic non-Christian claim is grossly misleading. Tolerance is a fundamental characteristic of Oriental religion but this is a tolerance born out of religious relativism which rejects any knowledge of truth as absolute. Consequently the unity tolerance espouses is a relativistic unity. Tolerance charges Christianity with intolerance because Christians proclaim a truth (God in Christ) which is absolute. In reality, oriental religion is intolerant about its own relativism and strives to coax Christians away from their "intolerant Gospel" and adopt the "intolerant relativism" of the East. The choice, therefore, is between two "intolerants," an "Absolute Gospel" or an "absolutized relativity." It is not necessary to enlarge on the point that Christians must accept, in the Spirit of the Gospel, the fact of differences in other religions without questioning the religious sincerity of those who hold them and, again, in the name of their Lord, must reject any approach of compulsion.

The Gospel, Christianity and Religion

If there is a great gulf between the non-Christian faiths and the divine revelation in Christ, then in the knowledge of that fact, Christians may discover more truly the discrepancy covery may tend to keep the whole issue of the relationship between Christianity and paganism in true perspective, out of the realm of controversy and pride. From the "religio of God" (Luther), the Gospel Word, the one True Religion, all religions of men are to be differentiated. The Gospel is the between the Gospel and empirical Christianity. Such a dis-judgment upon all religion, including Christianity. Any form of empirical Christianity which sets itself up as the one true infallible Church, beyond the judgment of the Gospel, does not "proclaim the Gospel but rather displaces it." Faith in the Gospel is the message of Christendom to all world faiths, world cultures, world crises. The radical opposition is not between paganism and Christianity but between paganism and Christianity's message. There is a solidarity of all religions in a condition of sin before the judgment seat of Christ, Brunner declares.

Now this has special significance for the Catholic Church of Christ as it faces the ecumenical problem under discussion. Some of the failure of Christianity in the non-Christian world lies in the fact that it has not always clearly understood and made evident this distinction in its evangelistic mission. And because that is so the non-Christian world has accused, rightly or wrongly, the Christian Church of "religious imperialism," trying to conquer or displace non-Christian faiths with particular brands of Christianity. Because Christ has instituted the Church to be the body of his witness in the world, Christianity faces a special judgment upon its life whenever or wherever it has made unbelievable the proclamation of the Gospel entrusted to it. One service which the non-Christian faiths may render the Church in its encounter with them, is to shake up the Church into being an authentic bearer of the Gospel message. On the other hand, the service which Christianity may render to other faiths, is to present them with the opportunity to behold Christ as the fulfillment of their deepest needs. Jesus Christ lifted up, is the hope of the Church and the hope of the world. He not only is the redeemer of individual lives but of individual cultures. The Church's greatest service is "to erect signs all over the world from which the message of the Gospel can be read." (Frick)

Though Christianity can be identified with other religions in its polarity to the Gospel, and because of that inevitably comes under judgment, there is a profound sense in which it is distinctive. Unlike other religions Christianity has been continuously in relationship with the Gospel. It is the religion of the Gospel. Wherever members of the Christian family set about quarreling among themselves over matters of faith and life, they still have a "listening post" between them because they all know themselves to be under the sovereignty of the Word. There can be continuous religious conversation because of the unbroken continuity with the Gospel.

In the diagram of H. Frick in *The Gospel, Christianity, and Other Faiths,* if one takes the Gospel as the center of religious reality, Christianity alone extends in radius from the circumference to the center. However imperfectly, empirical Christianity does live in direct communication with the Gospel and is its servant in the world. Because the Church is founded upon that Gospel and charged with the responsibility for broadcasting it, the Church must enter into active and intelligent dialogue with all non-Christian faiths in order that "the light of the Gospel may shine before men and the Father in heaven be glorified."

5

THE WORLD MISSION
OF THE CHURCH

A few years ago the slogan "Let the Church Be the Church" was quite popular in ecumenical circles. Slogans, of course, come and go, but the truth of slogans must not pass away. The truth is that the Church was not called into existence primarily to *say* or *do* something but to *be* something. When the Gospel became religion it was "established" much as education was instituted in the school. Though this "incorporation" was inevitable and necessary to its continued existence, it was never intended that the Gospel should be imprisoned in the institution. The Church was meant to be the redeeming community of Christ out in the world and only secondarily an institution. Much of the time of history has been given over to developing and solidifying the institution, cleansing it of heresy and abuse from within and defending it from attack without, and all of it vitally important. Meanwhile, its ministry of being the redemptive community in the world was weakened and, at times, even overlooked. The Gospel was "out of grips" with the world and the world fell farther away. The clearest symbol of spiritual reawakening today is the Church's fresh awareness of the world. Just as the school sees the need for extension courses offered on a broad scale, so the Church must be a ministering community in business, labor, government, professions, the arts, communication, in short, literally everywhere in the world.

In a recent, most provocative little book, Hendrik Kraemer

points up this character of the Church. "Her being an institution is a human necessity but not of the nature of the Church . . . But the Church should consciously affirm its charismatic above its institutional nature." [1] It is increasingly more evident that sharp distinctions between "home" missions and "world" missions or "missions" and "Mission" are untenable and misleading. Whether we are talking about the distance between the Gospel and pagan society in a modern Tokyo or the great divorce between the Gospel and contemporary American life, we are speaking essentially of the same thing. It is the conflict between the word of God and a world still without God. The Church's mission is to *be,* in reality, itself in the name of Christ, for the sake of the world. Over and beyond the discussion of the relation between Christianity and non-Christian faiths (which must be continuously carried on and deeply) is the larger discussion of the Gospel in a Gospel-less world. "God so loved the world"—this stupid, confused, selfishly-oriented, tragically separated world—that in Christ he came to reconcile it. The pity is that the world loves the darkness rather than the light.

In our first lecture we spoke of a world indifferent to the Gospel (though not religiously inactive), a world of change, confusion, and conflict which has seen the breakdown of community and communication suffering from spiritual nostalgia and homesickness. What is this but the stark evidence that the world remains unconquered, and largely unpenetrated by the Good News of God? Therefore, "O Zion, haste, thy mission high fulfilling . . . Tell how He stooped to save his lost creation." The Church must not become so lost in techniques, institutional machinery (necessary though it be), schemes and programs, that it loses sight of its call to be the Master's Mission in the redemption of the world.

[1] Hendrik Kraemer, *Theology of the Laity,* p. 181.

The secularistic world against which we preachers have hurled so many badly-aimed darts needs to be examined very thoroughly in the context of our preaching, pastoral ministry and church programs. The world's "gospel," because it has appeared to be more sensible and successful than the Christian "brand," may offer a subtle temptation to the Church to trim its Gospel down to become less of an offense. Norman Vincent Peale's efforts to baptize into the Church the world's prescription for meeting man's need for forgiveness, acceptance and meaning may reflect dramatically the Church's own failure to offer the Gospel concretely and relevantly to man in his predicament.

The modern worship of the scientific method and the idolizing of scientific achievements may simply be science's way of paying the Church back in kind for the theological and dogmatic blunders of an earlier day. Only now may there faintly be emerging a religious recognition of the justifiable autonomy of the scientific method. Perhaps the way may be cleared for the development of a full philosophy of science, broadened enough to give a larger role to imagination and intuition within its own discipline, and consecrated enough to see scientifically-arrived-at truth in the spectrum of the totality of truth, and God the all-including Truth.

The failure to reach the laboring classes with the Gospel —and the reason why labor unions, for some, have become a modern "principality and power"—may be largely the result of a class-conscious Church committed, on that particular issue, to a definite status quo philosophy. The Church's attitude to the so-called "right to work laws" may in a significant measure determine whether the Gospel gets to the laborer through the Church.

The tyranny of American education by "Deweyism" with its preoccupation with utilitarian ends of efficiency and success is only now beginning to wane in power in institutions of higher education though not appreciably in lower public education. The loss of spiritual ends in education cannot be separated from a narrow religiosity and religious parochialism in the churches.

The Christian pulpit and the pastoral ministry must be critically reexamined. Christian preaching is not always clearly distinguishable from the moralistic addresses semipiously delivered on public occasions and on TV broadcasts. There is a "hue and cry" for a return to great "biblical and doctrinal" preaching to put to flight the popularizing topical preaching on sundry topics, especially those suggested by last week's popular journals or editorials, and about which the hearers usually know far more than the preachers. But that very "doctrinal" preaching may end up being nothing more than interesting exegesis or clever doctrinal shavings instead of relevant divine Good News. The Good News may even turn up on Sunday morning as "no news" at all, or antiquated news, a contradiction of terms. The "good old Gospel" is often a biblical anachronism.

Secularism ought to be a wholesome catharsis for the Christian pulpit. When we are honest with ourselves we know how badly we have done. Hitting the homiletical doldrums, if not too oppressive, may be the beginning of a new life in our preaching. When the urge to toss away all our back sermons comes over us, it may be the first bright optimistic sign of renewal. How much of our week-to-week preaching has been planned carefully enough and executed not only to present the fullness of the Gospel message (not a homiletical monotone), but more importantly, specific enough to be relevant to the needs of worshippers? How often we preachers have waxed eloquent on solutions to social and world problems by the use of broad theological generalizations, with little understanding of the complexity of the issues or the circumstances surrounding them! It may very well be that much contemporary preaching is carried on in a vacuum where the message either sails over the heads or runs right on past the worshippers. Were it not for the total experience of worship many would go home empty.

No less a danger to communication lurks in our pastoral ministry. Conceivably the greatest incentive for congregations to obtain more money could be a primary one of "liberating" ministers, liberating them from an increasing preoccupation with administrative functions that they may return again to the "ministry of persons." There is a vast need to take time with people as Jesus did. The disciples were quite modern. They wanted to get on with the business. But Jesus had time to minister. He was pressed but never rushed. And it is surprising how much time he had for the little people.

He took time also to train his disciples. A. B. Bruce with keen insight, entitles his book *The Training of the Twelve.* Jesus' life may well be viewed in that light. He trained them not to face the world but to change the world. And the record says they turned the world upside down. How much time is spent in rearguard action counselling people on how to cope with the world; how little time is spent in vanguard action, preparing them for redeeming the times.

Secularism may well be the spur needed for the minister to see his role not only as spokesman and counsellor, but also teacher. The minister is called upon as never before to teach. Our primary task is to train the laity. If we really wish to do something about the nemesis of secularism, one thing we can do is to throw all our ingenuity, training and consecration into a "depth job," preparing the laity for responsible witness in the world right where they are, both in time and interest, most of the while. "Accepting Jesus Christ as Lord and Saviour" is not the answer to God's problem with the world. It is only part of the answer. It is the calling of a committed, informed band of laymen into a meaningful, redeemed community and then dispersing them into the world. We might let some of our Church programs die for the sake of it. Some of them are dead anyhow, they just haven't been buried. Such an economy of time and energy may enable the minister to concentrate on the preparation of these latter day disciples for the world.

How deep the inroads of secularism into our parish activities! How different in character are our congregational organizations from comparable groups outside the Church which have luncheon clubs, women's societies and youth agencies? One church organization was thrown into confusion when the minister innocently asked, "Now what is the main purpose of your group?" "Bake sales," "fish and chips," "lawn fetes" and "volunteer fire department" style carnivals, all need to be weighed against the Christian standard of stewardship. The secularism the Church inveighs against may turn out to be not too different from the secularism the Church adopts, save for the fact that in the world it is wiser than that of the children of light.

We may now give attention to the lines along which the Church must carry out its Mission to a lost world. None of it can be said to be new. But we must look afresh at the Gospel and the world it was meant for, in order that we may see ever anew the nature of our witness to the world and some of the principles of approach and action which ought to be followed. This holds for both the world we label Christendom, which largely belongs to another power, and the world we know to be non-Christian. There is a remarkable sameness about them. Though we must keep them separate in our thinking, they cannot in essence be divorced. They are both the problem of the universal Church and the mind of the whole Church must be fastened on them.

Art of listening

A sound principle of Mission as the Church moves into the realm of other religions and irreligion is listening. Here the Church can take a cue from the art of counselling. A good counsellor before he gives advice or directs his patient toward a constructive course of action, "hears the patient out." He must learn as much about the patient as he can. He says very little and when he does speak it is most often in the form of careful questioning which serves not only to get at the most important facts but also to help the patient himself to accept the solution. The counsellor cannot solve the patient's problem for him even when he sees clearly the solution. Until the patient himself is brought to the point where he can accept the answer, the problem remains unresolved.

To reject outright the religious faith of others or to condemn summarily irreligion is to conclude that nothing can be gained from listening. But unless we listen, the "patient" cannot be helped. He remains in a "stand off," even hostile, position. The Gospel is never accepted in an atmosphere of controversy. Besides, there is much to be gained in a full knowledge of the opposition. The rejection of the Gospel may be due to misconceptions in the minds of its rejectors. The fact that Christ is judge over contemporary Christianity arouses interesting thoughts about the rejection of Christianity by other faiths. What is it that they reject? Kraemer raises penetrating questions: "Is it Christ they reject or our interpretation of him? Are we Christians guilty of offering them the idol of Christ which we have made for ourselves and which they do not regard as authentic? Is it Christ or our Western, organized, activist, divided Christianity they reject?" [2] But we shall not know without patient listening.

[2] *Ecumenical Review*, January, 1957, p. 129.

Why do people remain outside the Church in America and Europe? Why is the Gospel not accepted by those within the Church? Granted that the Gospel is always an offense and for that reason meets with "failure," may not some of the failure be due not to the offense of the Gospel at all but to deep-seated psychological or sociological factors in the environmental make-up of the rejectors, or perhaps, to "offensive" Christians or an offensive Church? But how shall we know without listening? There is much we must learn about a secularistic world and we may need to withhold our message till our listening has provided for us a way. Much of the effectiveness of the German Evangelical Academies lies in a creative silence where as yet uncommitted laymen resolve the problems faced in their separate occupations.

Pastors and Christian lay leaders must step over into these frontiers of irreligion, where there will be no self-assertion in their witness but rather a teachable humility born out of gratitude to God and a selfless love for those of no-religion or other-religion whom God also loves. Until we learn to think and feel as they do by entering into their experiences we shall not be prepared to speak, in terms which they will understand, of what God has done for us and them. Was not one of the principal marks of Jesus' ministry that he listened to peoples problems, "heard them out," even over the impatience of some of the disciples, until they knew that he had identified them as his own? He knew what was in men and died for their reconciliation.

Understanding and appreciation

The nineteenth century produced a few giants among the missionaries of the stature of William Carey in the understanding of world religions, but by and large the early missionary movement little understood and perhaps little cared to know the religious and cultural heritage of the non-Christian world. Their purpose, a primary and noble one, was the evangelization of lost souls. Other things took a subordinate position and became relatively unimportant. As a consequence many of the early missionaries had to preach and teach through interpreters, most of whom were quite inadequately prepared for the task. This handicap has not yet been completely overcome. Until the language barrier is erased and people are taught in their own tongue, the Gospel will continue to suffer. Communication is essential to the intelligent understanding and appreciation of native culture as well as to the effectiveness of the Christian World Mission. Present day missionaries are required to learn the language though not all receive adequate preparation academically in the thought and culture of the land. And they are quick to admit it. Increasingly, furloughs are becoming, not rest periods (which they never were!), but opportunities for intellectual stimulation and growth, both in the knowledge of Christianity and the competitors of our Faith.

Yung-ch'ing Yang, in his *China's Religious Heritage,* observes that all the peoples of the world have their "father "Jacobs" from whose wells they have drunk for many years. One of the reasons Jesus could be so effective in dealing with the woman at the well of Jacob was that this woman was conscious that Jesus knew everything about her. We may not be prone to accept some of the compromising and radical turns of the Roman Catholic Church in its philosophy of Christian Mission but there are clear evidences that, in some respects, it has been better informed and thus better prepared than the Protestant community to deal with the non-Christian World. Some Catholic works, for example, on Mahayana Buddhist philosophy have been most perceptive and highly acclaimed.

One of the weaknesses in the Christian approach to the

Moslems has been the tendency to attack Islam as a false religion and Mohammad as a false prophet with the resulting controversy and counter attack from the Moslem community. More effort might have been spent in trying to understand the Moslem's inner longings, what his religion, in reality, is to him, and an appreciation of the Moslem's life of prayer and devotion. The Qur'an has been used too often by Christians simply for controversial or apologetic purposes with little regard for what is of real value in it. One can only rejoice in the establishment of Study Centers or Institutes like the Henry Martyn School of Islamic Studies in India, the International Institute for the Study of Religions in Tokyo, the Institute For the Study of Hinduism in Madras and similar centers for Buddhism in Ceylon and Burma.

If people are to be "saved by Christ" they will be saved in the context of their own culture and national environment. And they will be dispersed as "little christs" to that cultural soil in which they grew up and know to be theirs. How essential is a knowledge of and appreciation for that "soil" and heritage on the part of the Church!

Religious intercommunication

In speaking of religious intercommunication, I refer to voluntary channels of intercommunication between Christianity and Buddhism, Christianity and Hinduism, Christianity and Islam. This almost virgin territory is a very difficult and to some degree treacherous road to travel. It can also result in a quite superficial activity, depending on what grounds it is done and how. "The danger is, however, that such groups come and work together on the basis of the so-called disagreements and thus are unintentionally insincere." [3] Generally, Christianity and other religions have

[3] Kraemer, *Religion and the Christian Faith*, p. 367.

maintained a rigid apartness from each other. Yet the constraint of the Gospel, or if not that the demand for understanding, especially in this 20th century, should call for a sincere inquiry into what is truth or what constitutes the highest truth.

The fact is, there is intercommunication in all other respects. One of the signal characteristics of this century is that we know far more about the people of the world than we ever knew before. We have recognized the importance of intercommunication in politics, international relations and general culture. We have become better informed about the educational and social conditions and problems confronting the peoples of the world. Yet there is a regrettable block in intercommunication between religions.

I think Christianity could well recall the lessons learned in the growth of the ecumenical movement and the establishment of the World Council of Churches. For many years, denominations maintained their separateness, their apartness, without looking seriously at each other. Whatever the reasons, they continued their independent ways until in the course of events, conditions in the world, and more important, fast moving conditions within the Church, compelled denominations to reexamine their faith and life together.

Now obviously, there is a deep difference between divisions within a faith communicating with each other and one religion facing another. And a Christian's loyalty is always to Christ and him alone. Nevertheless, the great commission demands the greatest dialogue possible and religious intercommunication affords an important possibility. Indian Ashrams—communal experiments—in which people live together in conversation and communication, serve a good purpose though they may run the danger of syncretism. In Bangalore, Devanandan's Institute for the Study of Society is the kind of movement which not only seeks to relate the

Christian message to the problems of Indian society but provides, as well, for an encounter with non-Christian minds. [4] We have referred already to other institutes and research centers.

Such experiments do not mean the compromise of the Christian faith nor the diminishing of an intelligent, aggressive evangelism. It does mean, however, that the Gospel has a chance to meet, in a significant way, the great religions of the East. It is no disservice to the Truth of God in Christ. It may be, that for many it is the only way the Gospel may be made known, by word and by life. Perhaps there is an unnecessary hesitancy on the part of the Christian community to initiate such movements with other religions. The hesitancy may stem from a sense of inadequacy but it must be kept in mind that the Gospel in such encounter is not on trial. The truth of the Gospel is not validated or invalidated in any human court. And encounter is not fighting a case. It is bearing a witness. People are brought to Christ, not by our arguments, but by the power of the Holy Spirit.

A new kind of evangelism

Our day calls for an intellectual presentation of the Gospel. William Hocking writes: "The missionary movement has shirked the labor of thought. It has addressed the multitude, the poor and the outcaste, as it should have done; but it has avoided the scribes and Pharisees as it should not have done. To this extent it has been unworthy of its Master. It has not sought to save the world but only a fragment of the world." [5] An emotional concern for the lowly lost catapulted the Gospel to the far reaches of the earth. Christianity made its appeal to certain classes, particularly the uneducated

[4] Observations from one of our Indian missionaries.
[5] *International Review of Missions,* Vol. 1939, p. 385.

and oppressed. But the educated classes remained very largely outside the influence of the Gospel.

There is a new Christian adventure awaiting the Church, namely, the intellectual approach to evangelism. There are great intellectual frontiers which have never fallen before the Christian message. Christians may well ask themselves, "What has the mind of Christ to say to the whole modern mentality, modern ideologies, modern culture?" The genius of Reinhold Niebuhr and Paul Tillich, and their attraction for this twentieth century, rests in the fact that they have provided the kind of philosophical interpretation of Christianity which can give direction to this scientific, technological age. Men may debate their interpretations, reject, correct or modify some of their conclusions, but hardly can they deny their profound Christian influence upon contemporary culture.

In times past and today the Church has drawn the social implications of the Christian message. Hospitals, orphanages and other institutions of mercy were established at the command of the Gospel. Even new techniques for agricultural improvement were not considered foreign to the missionary task. The Gospel was "socialized." The time has come for the intellectualization of the Mission. The modern intellect must be mastered by the mind of Christ. "Love the Lord thy God with all thy mind."

Mind you, belief in God is not simply an intellectual matter. If that were all, Christianity would line up with the philosophies and become the possession of the few. It is a faith for all to declare and live by. It involves relationship and decision. It is not just a way of thinking. That is the error of the "so-called intellectual." Intellectuals rest on sofas in the evening endlessly discussing all the fine threads of philosophy and theology, and having aired them all, *ipso facto,* they are "religious." It costs nothing,—just "thinking."

It means no commitment, no sacrifice. Just think! I hold no brief for an "intellectualist religion." Thinking will not save the world. If it could, the world would have been saved many times over. I am simply saying that no religion can do its full work in this world without intensive, consecrated tools of thought. And thought at a high level!

The secret of the intellectual victory of Christianity—no mean victory!—over the organized and highly intellectualized pagan religions of the Greek world, was the rise within Christian circles of intellectual giants. It is time now for the Church to give birth to a new type of missionary. Not the pioneer missionary so needed in an earlier period. Not primarily the missionary evangelist (always needed) proclaiming the message of salvation in Christ. But the Christian thinker tackling the centers of learning, of intensified pagan learning (abroad or at home) with the mind and spirit of Christ. Religions and irreligion have thought behind them. It must be met with redemptive Christian thought.

Indigenous and interdependent Christianity

A Mission principle obvious to and accepted by every modern missionary is that of establishing an indigenous Christianity and Church; a Christianity as naturally at home in India or Africa as in the soil in which it first was planted, and planted again and again. Missionaries are quite aware of the claim that the Church in the East is still an "exotic, hot-house plant, protected from the native air rather than nourished by it." "Christianity is a Western religion," is a charge frequently leveled at the Church, by both friend and foe. Though the charge becomes less and less true as Christianity finds deeper rootage, it can hardly be denied as a fact. Indigeneity does not bloom overnight.

A truly indigenous Christianity is a profound spiritual

achievement. It begins with the overcoming of "foreignness." The shedding of paternalism, the taking over of responsibility and leadership, the securing of control, the power of self-support; these are some outward marks of a beginning of indigenization. They are by no means the real goal. The real sign is a maturation of a tradition. As one missionary beautifully stated it: "A tradition has to mature before an institution can produce leaders and reach a stage where it is critical enough to create, in the face of existing forms, its own *true* forms of expression." True leaders are not produced by outsiders (missionaries). They are produced by the tradition. Again, "It will be out of the fullness of the presence of the Church that an original art will become articulate. In the meantime, it is necessary that the evangelizers do not instill a dogma of form."

Another missionary expressed concern that while the Church gives "lip service to the indigenization of Christianity, it practices just the opposite." It fears mistakes and thus makes figureheads of native leaders. Quite obviously, there is raised here and elsewhere the practical problems of transition from the mission to the Church. It is easy to declare that the time has come for younger Churches everywhere to conduct their own affairs, but it is often very difficult, in fact, to leave major decisions to national leadership. As a world Christian leader put it: "In Asia we are at an end of *a* period *in* missions not at the end of *the* period *of* missions." [6]

"The sign of a universal religion," writes Hocking, "is that it can become particular." It can become particular without losing its universality. Here lies the genius of Christianity. It can become indigenous to any people yet not lose its universal character. Indeed, its universality lies largely in its particularization. The heart of autonomy is that each particular people may enter into a new and direct relationship to Christ as the head of the Church. As Chandran points out: "(Indigenization) is not a technique for evangelism but a necessary witness to the Incarnation of the Word of God." [7] The Word must be incarnated into every human situation even though it may be crucified in the process.

Nowhere must indigenization be more evident than in the theology of the Church. Its absence in the contemporary language of the people is one of the strongest denials of the catholicity of the Church. The younger Churches still bear here too many of the unmistakable marks of the sponsoring Western Church. Just as Augustine's use of Platonic philosophy to interpret Christian doctrine was a decisive factor in the Christianization of pagan thought and culture, though the god of Greek philosophy was not the God of Abraham, Isaac and Jacob nor the God of the Gospels, just so, there must arise in the contemporary Church of the non-Christian world, theologians of great stature who can in the thought forms of their own people interpret the saving Gospel of Jesus Christ. What possibilities can be made of such forms as avatars, bhakti, and yoga without the price of a compromising syncretism, remain still a dialectical question.

We have spoken of the urgent matter of indigenization. Indigenous seems to imply "independent" as over against dependent or paternal. There is another term which is far more accurate and Christian. It is the word "interdependent." No Christianity in any land ever becomes completely independent from Christianity elsewhere. One of the marks of Christianity is unity, and unity implies not independence but interdependence. There can be no completely independent Christianity, only interdependent Christianity. It is neither dependent nor independent. Rather it is both in-

[7] *Student World*, 4th Quarter, 1958, p. 341.

dependent and dependent. Christians are one in the en-
richment of faith and life.

Cooperation and unity

There seems not a little hypocrisy among some advocates
of other faiths who do not hesitate to point out the hopeless
disunity among Christians. "You come to us," they say,
"with the message of Christ and yet you are not agreed.
You are Presbyterians, Methodists, Baptists, Roman Catho-
lics, Lutherans, Seventh-Day Adventists, each professing to be
right, yet differing among yourselves."

The hypocrisy lies in the fact that there is not a religion
in the world which does not possess its divisions and differences. Every religion has divisions and sub-divisions. It is
true of Islam, Buddhism, Hinduism, and Shintoism. Yet the
truth in the charge is that divisions have often led to divisiveness and a fragmented message. Divisions have a natural
tendency toward exclusiveness, provincialism and "unholy
competition." It is the spirit of disunity or unholy competi-
tiveness which is the great sin of the Church, a sin of which
the Church must ever be aware and must somehow overcome. Though disunity is less a fact among Christians in
the non-Christian world, nevertheless the mission of the
Church has suffered irreparable damage not only through
the divisive spirit which does exist but also by the fact of
divisions themselves.

It is a matter of considerable joy and hope that one sees
developing at mid-century a greater movement toward unity
and cooperation among Christians in mission lands. There
are wholesome, intelligent movements toward church union
taking place in the midst of the pagan world. The formation
of the United Church of South India in 1947 and the present serious conversations between Lutheran bodies and that

Church looking toward merger is a source of great encouragement. The South India Church must be considered a *real* church, not a mere amalgamation of episcopal and non-episcopal bodies. It feels and acts like a Church. The very existence and vitality of the International Missionary Council and the close correlation of its functions with the World Council of Churches attests to the cooperation of the constituent denominational bodies.

Still, at a time, when for the sake of an effective evangelism Christianity must be fully prepared to meet a renascent paganism, Christian divisions present specially difficult problems. Not that unity should be considered a strategy for the sake of mission. It is a vital part of the mission itself. Yet every opportunity must be seized to overcome "the indifference, ignorance and rivalry which so often mark the Church's evangelistic witness." Churches must pray for and with one another and maintain the lines of mutual concern which by the Holy Spirit can be used to lead all Christians into a fuller knowledge of their oneness in the body of Christ. True Christian unity is far more than ecclesiastical oneness. It is a deep common life together, a radical partnership in Christ.

Certain virtues are particularly demanded in these difficult days of the Church's Mission, such as unsimmering enthusiasm, concentration, selflessness. Patience is another. To recognize that though Christ is the Church's message and the hope of the world, it may be a long, long while before that message and hope are accepted or even graciously considered. This calls for an unusual degree of patience. It calls, too, for courage. It calls for what the Evanston Conference spoke of as "identification," or that strange word "alongsidedness," where the Christian so identifies himself with the non-Christian, so becomes part and parcel of the non-Christian world, that he becomes totally one with his community and loses himself fully in it. He is no longer, therefore, a visitor, no longer a stranger from an alien land and culture. He is immersed, "baptized into the culture," becomes one with it and so identifies himself with it. Perhaps, just that virtue of alongsidedness is the one trait to dispel the stigma of "exclusiveness" leveled at the Christian faith and its modern bearers.

BIBLIOGRAPHY

Christianity and Secularism

AUBREY, EDWIN E. *Secularism A Myth*, Harper, 1954.

BAYNE, STEPHEN F. *The Optional God*, Oxford, 1953.

BOYD, MALCOLM. *The Crisis in Communication*, Doubleday, 1957.

CASSERLEY, J. V. L. *The Retreat From Christianity*, Longmans, Green, 1952.

CASSERLEY, J. V. L. *The Bent World*, Oxford, 1955.

HARKNESS, GEORGIA. *The Modern Rivals of the Christian Faith*, Abingdon, 1952.

HERBERG, WILL. *Protestant-Catholic-Jew*, Doubleday, 1955.

KRAEMER, HENDRIK. *Communication of the Christian Faith*, Westminster, 1956.

KRAEMER, HENDRIK. *The Theology of the Laity*, Westminster, 1959.

LOEW, CORNELIUS. *Modern Rivals to the Christian Faith*, Westminster, 1956.

LOWRY, HOWARD. *The Mind's Adventure*, Westminster, 1950.

NIEBUHR, H. RICHARD. *Christ and Culture*, Harper, 1951.

OSBORN, RONALD E. *The Spirit of American Christianity*, Harper, 1958.

PITTENGER, W. NORMAN. *Christ in the Haunted Word*, Seabury Press, 1953.

PITTENGER, W. NORMAN. *The Christian Way in the Modern World*, Cloister Press, 1944.

READ, DAVID H. C. *Communication of the Gospel*, Student Christian Movement Press, 1952.

RHODES, ARNOLD B. editor. *The Church Faces the Isms*, Abingdon, 1958.

SELDES, GILBERT. *The Great Audience*, Viking Press, 1950.

SPANN, J. RICHARD. *The Christian Faith and Secularism,* Abingdon, 1948.

TILLICH, PAUL. *The Protestant Era,* University of Chicago Press, 1948.

WALSH, CHAD. *Campus Gods on Trial,* Macmillan, 1953.

WEDEL, THEODORE. *The Christianity of Main Street,* Macmillan, 1950.

WHYTE, W. H. *The Organization Man,* Simon & Schuster, 1956.

WICKHAM, E. R. *The Church and the People in an Industrial City,* Lutterworth.

Christianity and Non-Christian Faiths

BOUQUET, ALAN C. *Christian Faith and the Non-Christian Religions,* Harper, 1958.

BRUNNER, EMIL. *Christianity and Civilization,* Nisbet & Co., 1948.

COOMARASWAMY. *Hinduism and Buddhism,* Philosophical Library, 1943.

DEWICK, EDWARD C. *The Christian Attitude to Other Religions,* Cambridge University Press, 1953.

FARMER, HERBERT H. *Revelation and Religion,* Nisbet & Co., 1954.

FORMAN, CHARLES W. *A Faith for the Nations,* Westminster, 1957.

FRICK, HEINRICH. *The Gospel, Christianity and Other Faiths,* Oxford, 1938.

HOCKING, WILLIAM E. *Rethinking Missions; A Layman's Inquiry,* Harper, 1932.

HOCKING, WILLIAM E. *Living Religions and a World Faith,* G. Allen & Unwin, 1940.

HOCKING, WILLIAM E. the *Coming World Civilization,* Harper, 1956.

JURJI, EDWARD J. *The Christian Interpretation of Religion,* Macmillan, 1952.

JURJI, EDWARD J., editor. *The Great Religions of the Modern World,* Princeton University Press, 1947.

KRAEMER, HENDRIK. *The Christian Message in the Non-Christian World,* International Missionary Council Publication, 1938.

KRAEMER, HENDRIK. *Religion and the Christian Faith,* Westminster, 1956.

LATOURETTE, KENNETH S. *The Christian World Mission,* Harper, 1954.

MANIKAM, RAJAH B., editor. *Christianity and the Asian Revolution,* Friendship Press, 1954.

MORGAN, KENNETH W., editor. *The Religion of the Hindus,* Ronald Press, 1953.

NILES, D. T. *The Preacher's Task,* Harper's, 1958.

NORTHROP, F. S. C. *The Meeting of East and West,* MacMillan, 1949.

PERRY, EDMUND. *The Gospel in Dispute,* Doubleday, 1958.

RADHAKRISHNAN, S. *Contemporary Indian Philosophy,* G. Allen & Unwin, 1952.

RADHAKRISHNAN, S. *Eastern Religions and Western Thought,* Oxford, 1939.

RADHAKRISHNAN, S. *The Hindu View of Life,* G. Allen & Unwin, 1927.

RADHAKRISHNAN, S. *Religion and Society,* G. Allen & Unwin, 1947.

TOYNBEE, ARNOLD. *An Historian's Approach to Religion,* Oxford, 1956.

TOYNBEE, ARNOLD. *Christianity Among the Religions of the World,* Scribner, 1957.

WORLD COUNCIL OF CHURCHES. *Six Ecumenical Studies for Evanston Conference.*

Type used in this book
Body, 11 on 13 Baskerville
Display, Baskerville
Paper: R.R.R. Standard White Antique